W9-BHV-256

THE
FALL OF FRANCE,
1940

PROBLEMS IN
EUROPEAN CIVILIZATION

Under the editorial direction of
John Ratté
Amherst College

The Fall of France, 1940

Causes and Responsibilities

Second Edition

Edited and with an introduction by

Samuel M. Osgood
Kent State University

D. C. HEATH AND COMPANY
Lexington, Massachusetts Toronto London

Copyright © 1972 by D.C. Heath and Company.
Also copyright 1965 by D.C. Heath and Company.

All rights reserved. No part of this publication may be reproduced or transmitted in any form or by any means, electronic or mechanical, including photocopy, recording, or any information storage or retrieval system, without permission in writing from the publisher.

Published simultaneously in Canada.

Printed in the United States of America.

International Standard Book Number: 0-669-81661-2

Library of Congress Catalog Card Number: 72-1851

CONTENTS

INTRODUCTION

"La France ne peut pas mourir," proclaimed Paul Reynaud at the conclusion of a radio address announcing Italy's declaration of war on
June 10, 1940. Those of us who heard the original broadcast remember that the weariness and anguish in the French Premier's voice
belied his brave words.[1] Coming a month to the day after the beginning of the German offensive, Mussolini's "stab in the back" was
but the *coup de grâce* to an already mortally wounded France.

In retrospect, the most striking thing about the fall of France was
the suddenness and thoroughness of it all. Even Hitler's spectacular
successes in Poland, Denmark, Norway, Holland, Belgium, and Luxembourg had failed to prepare world public opinion for the complete
collapse of the France of Joffre, Foch, and Clemenceau. Memories of
1914 were still quite vivid, and one kept waiting for another "miracle
of the Marne." Besides, was not the Maginot Line impregnable? It
was with a sense of disbelief that one learned of the French surrender at Compiègne on June 22.

Paradoxically, the defeat of France came as less of a surprise to
her own people than it did to the world at large. The impression is
that of a stunned, drugged nation, docilely accepting the not unexpected outcome of a conflict that had never seemed real. The le-
thargic months of the "phony war" had done nothing to kindle the
martial fervor of a people who had shown a decided lack of enthusiasm in rallying to the flag. In September 1939 there had been
no equivalent to the *union sacrée* of August 1914. More than one
Frenchman shared the feeling of Jean Dutourd's Sergeant Cepi in

---

[1] Portions of this speech have been recorded in Edward R. Murrow's "I Can Hear
It Now," Vol. I (Columbia—ML 4095).

the face of defeat: "Well, that's that." Subsequent events would soon lead to less dispassionate reactions.

Today, the country faces fewer problems than at any time in its long and troubled history. The French Empire has been liquidated at last, and the smooth transfer of executive power from De Gaulle to Pompidou, in 1969, would seem to indicate that France may have found a working solution to her perennial political problem. Yet there is an undercurrent of bitterness ready to erupt at the least provocation. There have been precious few references to *la douce France* since 1945! This toughened outlook is the direct legacy of the events and developments of the period 1939 to 1945. Indeed, the loss of the Battle of France, the demise of the Third Republic, the consolidation of the Vichy Regime, Pétain's National Revolution, the ordeal of German Occupation, the Resistance Movement, the settling of accounts at the time of the Liberation, and the birth of the Fourth Republic are all parts of an organic whole. They all add up to one tremendous traumatic experience which has had deep and pervasive impact on today's France. Not the least interesting by-product of this experience is that the generation gap is wider in France than in most other countries. The men of the Resistance generation, who lived through it and have "a practical monopoly of the French Establishment" in days of unparalleled prosperity, are ill-prepared to understand their offsprings' strident accusations that something is rotten in contemporary French society.[2]

The general topic "France in World War II" readily suggests possible titles for a half-dozen problem books of this type. The present inquiry is centered on the historical debate over the defeat of France by Nazi Germany in the spring of 1940. What might appear to be an arbitrary delimitation of subject matter can be defended on a variety of grounds. First and foremost, the debacle of 1940 was the curtain raiser to, the opening wedge for, the series of chain reactions mentioned above. Of course one cannot rewrite history. It does seem highly probable, however, that but for the defeat, the enemies of the Third Republic would never have had an opportunity to bury

[2] David B. Goldey, "A Precarious Regime: The Events of May 1968," in Philip M. Williams, ed., *French Politicians and Elections, 1951–1969* (Cambridge, 1970), p. 227. The regime of the Fifth Republic is and was less "precarious" than it appeared to be in the wake of the events of May 1968, when Professor Goldey originally published his article. [Editor's note.]

Marianne, and to launch the National Revolution of their dreams. The Vichy Regime then begat the Resistance Movement, and the Resistance begat the blood bath of the Liberation. One could go on. The effects of such bitter experiences cannot be exaggerated. Second, there is the complexity of the question. During the Great War, as the First World War is still called in France, the *poilus* had won the respect and admiration of the world by their dogged courage and tenacity. In 1940, France went down like a lamb. In 1918, as the senior partner of a victorious coalition, France had seemingly settled accounts with her old German foe for a long time to come. Yet, some twenty years later, Hitler's legions were marching down the Champs-Elysées. How can one account for such a striking reversal in the fortunes of the nation? Was it the result of relentless and impersonal historical forces? Were the seeds of future defeat contained in a victory won at the unbearable cost of 1.5 million men in a country of some 39 million people? Had something been corroding and undermining the spirit of the French? Were men or institutions—or both—to blame? The historian facing up to such questions soon comes to the realization that they entail much more than mere military considerations. He cannot hope to find the approximation of an answer, much less to reach definite conclusions, without first weighing the relative importance of a host of political, economic, social, demographic, intellectual, and psychological factors.

Finally, there is the intensity of the debate. National calamities always engender bitter recriminations. This is especially true in a country where political differences have traditionally been deep and acute. Small wonder, then, that both the politicians of the Third Republic and the leaders of the Vichy Regime should have sat in turn at the bench of the accused. Here again, the historian seeking impartiality must work his way through a maze of accusations and counteraccusations, through charges of treason indiscriminately hurled by all sides. The complexity of his task is matched only by its fascination.

Since 1945, the population at large has been much more reluctant than its leaders to engage in the debate over the causes and responsibilities for the debacle of 1940. A poll taken by the *Sondage de l'Opinion Publique Française,* in June 1945, gives us a rare inkling of the rank-and-file Frenchman's verdict on an episode which he would understandably rather forget. The actual question was: "What, in your opinion, was the principal cause of the weakness of France in 1939?" According to Saul K. Padover: "The replies showed a bewildered national mind; 31 percent held that the French people were themselves guilty; 18 percent found the leaders guilty; 13 percent ascribed responsibility to politics in general; and the remainder cited treason, national disunity, the low birth rate, and a number of other causes. In answer to another questionnaire concerning the enfeeblement of France, 47 percent of the respondents held alcoholism responsible."[3]

One can only agree with Professor Padover that there is an element of truth in all of these answers. The question is, how much? How, for instance, does one weigh the importance of the role played by defeatists against the fact that France's labor force was but one-third of Germany's? The problem is all the more difficult because, as the texts included in this book will show, historians and other commentators have advanced as many reasons for the country's collapse as the French people themselves.

Professor John B. Wolf's, "The *Elan Vital* of France: A Problem of Historical Perspective" is presented by way of introduction. As the title indicates, this selection does not deal primarily with the events of 1939–1940. Yet it has profound bearing on the question because the author carefully delineates France's relative decline in modern times as a result of her failure to adapt to 19th and 20th century conditions. Unfortunately, the French people continued to think and act in terms of the mission of *la grande nation* after its *élan vital* had been sapped. The implicit conclusion is that Germany's victory in 1940 was the culmination of a long historical process.

The second section deals primarily with the political aspects of the problem. As might be expected, the debate is especially acrimonious in this area. While none of the traditional democracies emerged completely unscathed from the turmoil of the 1930s, the severest attack against parliamentary institutions and liberal values occurred in France. There, a numerically weak, but socially and economically important segment of the population advocated the overthrow, or at least the reform, of the Third Republic. There were few

[3] Saul K. Padover, "France Today," *Social Research,* XVI (December, 1949), p. 493.

out-and-out fascists in France, but the Right and Extreme Right manifested strong authoritarian leanings. The war was anything but popular in these circles, and their spokesmen were prompt to blame the regime for the defeat. The excerpts from Pierre Laval's speech of July 10, 1940, Marshal Pétain's speech of October 11, 1940, and Charles Maurras' Apologia (at his trial for "intelligence with the enemy," January 1945) add up to the classic Rightist thesis that a decadent and venal Republican Government plunged a morally, militarily, and diplomatically unprepared France into an unnecessary war that she could not possibly win. While not in any way pro-German, the tone of these witnesses is always Italophile and Anglophobe.

The Vichy Regime's abrupt cancellation of the trial of Republican leaders at Riom in 1942, before a verdict had been reached, is ample testimony that the latter were not without a rejoinder. Typical of their line of argumentation is the selection from Edouard Daladier's deposition before the postwar Commission of Inquiry. In measured tones, the former Prime Minister explains why his Government had no alternative save to go to war against Germany in September 1939. Another former premier, Paul Reynaud, whose fate it was to be in office from March to June 1940, develops the interesting theme that France was not defeated because of an excess of democracy, but *precisely* because the duly elected representatives of the people had long since surrendered their powers to the experts and technicians. Reynaud does not mince his words, and he is especially critical of Pétain's role and influence during the interwar period.

No treatment of the political aspects of the fall of France would be complete without consideration of the Communist Party's role in the affair. A distinct feature of French Communism has long been its utter subservience to directives from Moscow. Thus Maurice Thorez and his cohorts, who had been at the forefront of the "stop Hitler" movement, did a complete about-face after the signing of the Nazi-Soviet Pact. In fact, their antiwar attitudes and activities led to the Party's dissolution on September 26, 1939. In the next selection, A. Rossi, an outstanding Italian student of the French Communist Party, attempts to assess its responsibilities for the debacle on the basis of the best available evidence.

France's military and diplomatic policies in the face of an impending conflict have also given rise to much controversy, and are the subjects examined in the third section. The immediate impression, following the debacle, was that France had been overwhelmed by vastly superior, better equipped, and better trained German forces. Needless to add that this version was not seriously challenged by the top French military leaders. The publication of Colonel A. Goutard's book on the Battle of France, in 1956, represents a landmark in this area of the debate. Using an impressive array of statistics, as well as the testimonies of a number of German generals, the author argues that in terms of men and weapons, the French were more than a match for the Germans. The fault lay in obsolete doctrines (French military thinking had crystallized after 1918) and incompetent leadership. The French generals did not understand the most elementary rules of modern warfare, and failed either to make proper use of the weapons at their disposal or to exploit German mistakes and weaknesses. In this light, insofar at least as the Battle of France is concerned, World War II was indeed "the War of missed opportunities." Whether or not the reader agrees with General André Beaufre's bold assertion that "the collapse of the French Army is the most important event of the Twentieth Century," he will want to give careful consideration to his argument that there was nothing to be done by 1940. The odds against France were overwhelming. In the next selection John C. Cairns, a brilliant Canadian student of the question, expresses strong reservations about the Goutard thesis. Cairns feels that the debacle of 1940 cannot be really understood so long as it is considered solely as a French phenomenon. In his words, "the Armistice of June 25 was French, but the military collapse was European." According to Pierre Cot, the controversial Minister of Aviation of Popular Front days, the one overriding consideration was the breakup of the Franco-Russian Alliance. There could be no Battle of the Marne in 1940, because there was no Eastern Front.

The fourth section emphasizes the importance of intellectual, social, and psychological factors. As Pierre Drieu La Rochelle, a talented right-wing writer saw it, France was killed by an all-encroaching rationalism. Whatever the validity of Drieu La Rochelle's devastating indictment of French society, his views were shared by a number of highly influential intellectuals. His complaint about the subservience of the working class to orders from Moscow was often echoed by his fellow Rightists, who equated such a relationship with treason. Jean Dutourd, one of the wittiest novelists of contemporary France, points the finger of guilt at "the men of fifty." Overwhelmed by the glorious deeds of their fathers, the *poilus,* the men of the postwar generation, turned away from the challenges of their times and sought escapism in the pursuit of senseless pleasures. Alexander Werth, who ranks among the keenest observers of the French scene, was especially familiar with the attitudes and aspirations of the bourgeoisie during the interwar period. While he dismisses the theory of a deliberate plot against the regime (as do, today, all serious students of the period), Werth concludes that the ruling classes had no great enthusiasm for the war, and that they easily became reconciled to a defeat which would sweep away the hated parliamentary institutions. In contradiction to Drieu La Rochelle, Jacques Maritain comes stoutly to the defense of the French people. He argues that the failures of the General Staff and the statesmen should not be laid at the door of the average Frenchman, who showed throughout the ordeal that he had retained many of his traditional qualities.

Two selections are presented by way of conclusion in Section V. Edouard Bonnefous' article is an attempt at synthesis by a leading French student of the Third Republic. Marc Bloch, one of France's foremost medievalists and a martyr of the Resistance, surveys the whole question in magistral fashion. Not only does Bloch raise searching questions, but he also points the way to much needed further research. Since it makes no claim to have the final answers, the last selection in a sense typifies the spirit of this book. It is, in fact, much more of a beginning than an end. Hopefully, the selections below will prompt the thoughtful student to want to learn more about a crucial episode in the history of a country and a people who continue to puzzle friend and foe alike.

CONFLICT OF OPINION

The greatest crime committed in our country for many a year was certainly to declare war without adequate military and diplomatic preparations . . . . We are no longer a free people. Why? Because we made every mistake in the book.

PIERRE LAVAL

In truth, the disaster was simply the reflection, on a military plane, of the weaknesses and defects of the former regime. . . . One day in September, 1939, without even daring to consult the Chambers, the Government declared war. This war was all but lost in advance.

PHILIPPE PÉTAIN

We did everything in our power to prevent the outbreak of hostilities, because we were under no illusions as to the nature and meaning of modern war. We worked night and day to find an acceptable compromise. We went as far as was humanly possible. . . . I believed then as I do now . . . that France was initially capable of resisting, if not of invading and defeating Germany. . . . I did not for a moment envision the possibility of a military collapse.

EDOUARD DALADIER

France's misfortune was not that she was saddled with a Parliament, but that hers was not worthy of the name. . . . We were defeated because the parliamentary regime failed to function.

PAUL REYNAUD

. . . It was not the nation's 'pleasure-seeking' which forced the Command to cling to a doctrine which was out of date, to work out an erroneous plan of campaign, to adopt faulty general dispositions, and finally to allow itself to be constantly out-maneuvered by the enemy without attempting the least counter-stroke. And all this at a time when the chance of victory was actually there!

COLONEL A. GOUTARD

By 1940 there was nothing to be done: fate had stacked the cards too heavily against us.

GENERAL A. BEAUFRE

The more one looked the more one became convinced that this Strange Defeat would never be comprehensible considered solely as a French phenomenon. The Armistice of June 25 was French, but the military collapse was European.

JOHN C. CAIRNS

What was the basic difference between 1914 and 1939? The basic difference is that, in 1914, we were allied with both England and Russia. Without the Russian advance in East Prussia, we would never have been able to rally at the Marne. In 1939, we did not have the support of Soviet Russia. Nothing can obscure this fact.

PIERRE COT

France was destroyed by the rationalism to which her genius had been reduced.

PIERRE DRIEU LA ROCHELLE

It has repeatedly been said that France was betrayed in 1940. Of course she was betrayed. But not by the Fifth Column. She was betrayed by you, men of fifty. She was betrayed by what should have been her vital forces.

JEAN DUTOURD

I OVERVIEW

John B. Wolf

THE *ELAN VITAL* OF FRANCE: A PROBLEM OF HISTORICAL PERSPECTIVE

John B. Wolf (1907–), a long-time member of the faculty at the University of Minnesota, his alma mater, is currently Professor of History at the University of Illinois, Chicago Circle. While Professor Wolf is best known for his many publications in the early modern period, his France: 1814–1919 (now available in paperback) has won a lasting and well-deserved popularity. The author's perceptive analysis of the gradual decline of France's élan vital, after she had reached her apogee in the 17th and 18th centuries, will prove extremely useful to anyone seeking a long-range explanation for the collapse of 1940.

It would be easy for a discussion of the *élan vital* of France to degenerate into relatively meaningless and insignificant generalizations unless some criteria for analysis can be established. The usual meaning of the term is constrained by context, so that it is not very useful in a discussion dealing with an organic unit like a nation. Bergsonian philosophers, the revolutionary labor leaders, and the "Young Turks" in the French army personalized the conception and thereby narrowed it so that it hardly applies to a whole people. If, therefore, we are to arrive at any significant conclusions about the effectiveness and survival value of the French nation, we must associate the idea *élan vital* with the total psychological-biological process of its historical development in modern times. Only after we have applied the conception to the totality of French life can we profitably turn our attention to the more intimate problem of the *élan vital* of individuals or groups within the society.

When we focus our attention on the historical process, we must also avoid postulating a mysterious force, a spring of vital energy or drive, that somehow molds the evolution of a people. Such an assumption may be useful to patriotic orators on festive occasions, but even Rousseau never went so far in elaborating his General

From *Modern France*, ed. Edward Meade Earl (Princeton, 1951), pp. 19–31. Reprinted by permission of Princeton University Press.

Will, and the soberminded historian will be chary of such postulates. On the other hand, it seems reasonable to assume that the *élan vital* of a people can be judged by their ability to adjust their national life to the larger historical processes of the development of Western Europe. This assumption postulates a community, perhaps in the sense that Rousseau described it; it assumes that the community as a political-biological fact does develop in the same environment with other similar communities; and lastly it presupposes that there is a characteristic form of development in the larger community that can be used as a measuring stick. Since these are the hypotheses that every historian must assume if he is to discuss the rise of modern Europe, they are not unreasonable and they may be useful in our discussion.

There are several levels of achievement that we must consider. The most obvious is purely materialistic: does the community provide for the economic well-being of its people on a standard comparable with that maintained by other communities? The second is political: is the community sufficiently in agreement on the popular mythology and the fundamental aims of the group to assure homogeneity? In other words, is there a general will that can be implemented politically? A third level is psychological: do the people have confidence in their future and their destiny—a confidence strong enough to encourage them to maintain and increase their numbers, to induce them to take social and economic risks, and to impel them to defend their lands whatever the personal sacrifice? Lastly, does the vigor of the community lead to creative social and intellectual development? Obviously the answers to these questions must be relative to the larger processes in the European community if they are to measure the *élan vital* as we have described it.

Let us recognize at the outset that these criteria are loaded against the French. They ask no questions about spiritual well-being, about refinements in manners and morals, about *civilisation* as the French often use the term. Nor do they take into consideration the inner psychological fact that a man's success or failure, his happiness or misery, in the last analysis, depends upon his individual values and may well be quite independent of the destiny of the nation. However, by defining the community as the unit that we are to consider, we automatically reject the atomistic conception of society, and assume that all values ultimately stem from the organic development of the group. Without economic, political, and military stability, no society has long maintained either high standards of civilization or a creative social life.

Our criteria, even without further discussion, will warn anyone familiar with French history that there has been a serious decline in the *élan vital* of France. This discovery is not very startling; publicists and philosophers have been expressing it for half a century. But if we are to understand the forces underlying our problem, we must try to discover when this decline began so that we can assess the problem at hand. Many writers have assumed that the watershed is to be found somewhere in the first decade of the twentieth century; the fact that the Third Republic survived in spite of the hostility of its opponents is thus confused with underlying forces in the historical process. A better point of departure, if one is not too deeply committed to the *mystique* of 1789, is the era of the Revolution and the Empire. With the exception of a few years under the government of Louis Napoleon, the entire period since Waterloo has seen the progressive failure of the French to adjust their development to the process in the other advanced countries of Europe. In the period before the Revolution, France was a leader, perhaps *the* leader, in Europe; her curve of development set the standard for Western society. A cursory glance at the history of France in the last three centuries will give us the evidence we need.

The modern French state, as contrasted with the Medieval and Renaissance kingdom of France, is the creation of the seventeenth century. Henry IV, Richelieu, and Louis XIV were agents of the forces that gave characteristic form to the centralized, bureaucratic, military police state. The forms that came into being in the latter seventeenth century continued to assert themselves, to extend themselves, and to facilitate further development in the characteristic pattern even though the constitutional provisions of the country might indicate Monarchy, Empire, or Republic. Historical processes have a way of asserting their power to survive revolution and violence, and to control the development of characteristic form.

In the century and a half before the Revolution the *élan vital* of France was maintained at a very high level. That was an era in which the French—despite the social strains which precipitated the Revolution—were essentially in agreement about their social and political myths, and in which the economic structure of the Western world gave France relative advantages that maintained the standards of living and the economic vigor of the people. In this period the people were able to accept a common ideal: One God, One Law, One King over a society organized in social hierarchies that assured to each the privileges of his class and the economic status appropriate to the station in life to which God had called him. It is true that the *politique* of the society, to borrow Péguy's term, did not always correspond to this *mystique*. Vauban's famous report at the opening of the eighteenth century, for example, lifts the curtain to show dissatisfaction, distress, and misery. Nevertheless, in the same decade that Vauban wrote the *Dîme royale* (1707) the French people responded to Louis XIV's cry, "The Kingdom is in danger," and supplied Villars with the men, money, and material necessary to beat off a coalition of all Europe led by two of the foremost captains of modern times. The myths of a society often fit the facts but poorly; they do, however, establish the goals, and it is the essential unity of the aspirations and aims of a people that make them a people, not the events of a year or a decade.

From the moment that Henry IV claimed the throne to the fatal day on which Louis XVI lost it, Bourbon France suffered chronic financial malaise. The organization of the monarchy was such that it was almost impossible for the king to tap the wealth of the kingdom for the use of government. When one thinks of the burden of taxation of the old régime, this statement seems paradoxical; it is nonetheless true. Even a Sully or a Colbert was unable to reorganize the fiscal structure of the kingdom to correspond to the realities of economic life. The financial instability of the Bourbon kings, however, must not be regarded as evidence that France under the old régime was a poor country, economically behind her neighbors. Quite the contrary was true. France showed striking economic vitality throughout the seventeenth and eighteenth centuries. The sensational recoveries that followed both the disaster of the forty years of civil and religious warfare in the later sixteenth century and the depression resulting from the wars and the drought years in the last two and a half decades of Louis XIV's reign provide ample evidence of the essential soundness of French economy. Even the bad government of Louis XV could not check this growth or impair the confidence of the nation in its future. The *cahiers* that the deputies brought to Versailles in 1789 testify eloquently to the faith of the people; they recognized abuses and problems, but they were not beaten down by economic distress.

Nor was this fundamentally sound picture of the *élan vital* of the nation confined to economics and politics. Throughout most of the seventeenth and eighteenth centuries the French were the intellectual leaders of Europe. For only a few years at the opening of the eighteenth century the intellectual hegemony temporarily passed to the England of Newton, Locke, and the Augustine writers; by the mid-eighteenth century French astronomers, chemists, mathematicians, naturalists, and philosophers had regained the brilliant position that their forefathers had held under the *Roi Soleil*. French artists and architects took the place of the Italians in the last quarter of the seventeenth century as the leaders of Europe and maintained their position for two hundred years.

Obviously there were gross injustices in the society of the old régime, but this is not the place to pass judgment upon them. There were gross inequities, from the viewpoint of the twentieth century, in every society in Europe, and it would be difficult to prove that France under the Bourbons was strikingly worse than her neighbors. Indeed a strong argument might be made to show exactly the contrary. The France that so successfully stood off all Europe for twenty-five years after 1789 obviously was not a nation beaten to the ground by internal distress.

When we shift our attention to the France of the nineteenth century, the first thing that attracts our notice is the fragmentation that appears in the national will. The old myth, One God, One King, One Law, no longer compels loyalty; in its place we find slogans that proclaim programs: "Liberty, Equality, Fraternity"; "Equality, Order, Obedience"; "Social Justice"; "Property is theft"; "Workers of the world unite." The Revolution of 1789 shifted the axis of political life from the organic conception of the state to an atomistic one, and at the same time expanded the number of political wills to include all members of society. This sharp break with traditions opened wide the possibility of divergent political and social mythology, and granted to every group, indeed to every individual, the right to proclaim a program and to elevate it to the status of a political absolute.

The differences that appear in the course of the nineteenth century are fundamental; they imply a wide diversity of social and political goals and, indeed, mutually exclusive conceptions of God. Furthermore, the process of fragmentation was progressive; by the end of the century there were three major mythologies clamoring vehemently for supremacy, and within each of the major divisions, cults were beginning to appear further to atomize the national will. The crisis did not reach proportions implying the nonexistence of a General Will until the 1930s, but even by 1900 the seeds of the disaster were well sprouted. Unless the process is checked the General Will of the nation will be destroyed, leaving only particular wills and anarchy or tyranny as the ultimate result.

At the end of the seventeenth century Bishop Bossuet explained in his *Variations of the Protestant Churches* that the process of religious fragmentation must lead to indifference to God and anarchy in society. The Bishop's predictions were partially wrong, because he did not understand that the state could take the role that religion had traditionally played as the custodian of the beliefs and practices of the community. Were he to see the France of the early twentieth century with its variations in political cults, he would be sure that the Reformation was finally producing its fruit. The same process that had broken the Christian community of Europe in his day seemed to be at work to destroy the political community of France.

The dissociation on the political level was undoubtedly symptomatic of deeper forces at work in the society. This same nineteenth century saw French economy fall behind the developments in the other advanced nations of Europe. It saw the intellectual hegemony of the Continent pass to England and Germany. French artists cultivated flowers from their environment, a few distinguished individuals made great contributions to the science that the Western world was developing, but the creative political and economic forces that had made France paramount in the seventeenth and eighteenth centuries seem either to have lost dynamic power or to have been dissipated in fruitless controversy.

It is unnecessary to pile up evidence of the tragic failure of France to adjust herself to the emerging industrial-scientific society of the twentieth century, but it should be profitable to inquire into the underlying forces that were at work in the society. Perhaps we will be on firmer ground if we follow Goethe's admonition, *"Am Anfang war die Tat,"* and regard brute fact before we attempt to probe political or psychological processes.

France seems to have had little difficulty in adjusting herself to the historical processes of the seventeenth and eighteenth centuries. That was an era in which agriculture, commerce, and handicraft production dominated economic life. The masses made their living from the soil in villages that were relatively self-sufficient; manufacturing was largely confined to small enterprises employing few men; the commercial and financial entrepreneur was the representative of the capitalism of the period. It was a society that depended upon wind, water, and the backs of men and animals for power, and relied upon wood for its principal material. France was eminently fitted to function efficiently in such a civilization. Her soil was fertile, her climate mild, her agriculture as advanced as any in Europe and her peasants were industrious. The French craftsmen were skilled, and French merchants aggressive. Located so that her harbors faced both the Levant and the Atlantic, France enjoyed a favored position to compete for the commerce of the world.

Furthermore, the form of seventeenth and eighteenth century commerce was favorable to France. The market was weighted to cater to the needs of the wealthy in society, and therefore the items of luxury trade loomed relatively large in the total commerce. From the sixteenth century onward French manufacturing tended to emphasize the luxury trade; actually, even in the preceding two centuries this tendency was already in evidence. Fine wines, expensive textiles, jewelry, glassware, mirrors, and other articles *de luxe* were the products of France. Even at this early date there was a significant difference in the economies of France and England; the latter emphasized the workaday world—hardware, cheaper textiles, and other articles with relatively wide mass appeal—while the "finer things of life" came from France. The French reputation for quality was so great that certain English manufacturers shipped their products to France for re-export to England so that the goods could be marked "Made in France." Seventeenth- and eighteenth-century France thus was admirably suited to function efficiently in Europe.

The economy of the kingdom was well within the norm of European development; even the regulations that Bourbon kings placed upon commerce and manufacturing in their effort to use economic life as a state-building process was characteristic of the whole European picture.

In the nineteenth century, however, France progressively lost the favorable position that she had enjoyed earlier. This was an age of coal and iron and science, and the center of gravity of the market shifted from luxury items to capital goods and commodities for mass consumption. By the opening of the twentieth century the great industrial machine, using enormous quantities of power and substituting the laboratory for the skill of the craftsman, became the characteristic form for European economy.

France was ill-equipped to adjust herself to this new economic process. Her beautiful countryside was lacking in the one essential commodity: coal. At no time after 1815 did the domestic production of coal satisfy the total demand. This fact meant that she was in no position to exploit her great deposits of ferrous metals, since these minerals normally move to coal for efficient production. France did develop heavy industry; she did build factories and foundries comparable to those of her neighbors, but she was unable to do so on the same scale as Britain and Germany. The handicap in fuel made her competitive position hazardous and prevented her from achieving the productive capacity of her neighbors. This fact brought another problem in its train: French industry was not equipped to make full use of the science that was transforming the face of the economy of Europe. Only large enterprises could afford to maintain the expensive laboratories that were developing new processes and new commodities. This in turn affected the educational system, for without the market for engineers and scientists, the French technical schools fell behind those of Germany, England, and the United States. In the eighteenth century French technical education was second to none; in the nineteenth and twentieth centuries it lagged behind. This lack of coal and comparative inability to utilize scientific information left France in a disadvantageous position in the economic society of the West.

While she fell behind in the race for heavy industry, her position in the luxury trades seemed secure. The tendency in human behavior to extend a mode of action is nowhere better illustrated than in the emphases on luxury production in France. French workers had an advantage in this traffic, and in turn strengthened their ability to extend their markets. It was a traffic that eminently fitted the skill and the temperament of the French artisan class, and this facilitated the further development of the industry. In the nineteenth century when machine-made and shoddy were almost synonymous, the luxury industry could easily support the hand-worker and even assure him an advantageous position in the market, but in the twentieth century when the gap between machine- and hand-quality narrowed, the French artisan as well as his employer faced a crisis, a relative decline in the value of their products. Furthermore, the emphasis on luxury goods worked another disadvantage upon the nation. In the twentieth century the ability to produce steel and sulphuric acid counted more in a contest of military and political power than the ability to produce a subtle perfume or a lady's hat. The world that was making bigger and better guns, bigger and better atom bombs, even bigger and better hogs and cows, had small favor for a society that emphasized uniqueness, artistry, and personal skill. These are values that pay dividends in personal satisfaction, but they count little in the play of power in the modern world.

Agricultural progress in the nineteenth century was not much more encouraging. French farmers resisted change during the whole period. In spite of the freedom granted by the Revolutionary legislation, the change from old to new methods of agriculture was painfully slow, and by the time that methods grounded in the Middle Ages were largely eradicated, [in other countries] startling new developments in agriculture . . . again left the French peasants far behind. In the last quarter of the century rural France received a terrible blow. New methods of transportation brought the cheaply produced foodstuffs of the Americas to Europe on a heretofore inconceivable scale, at the very time when pests and disease blighted French fields. Land values that had reached a peak under Napoleon III were cut in half, and large tracts of French agricultural land became submarginal. The readjustments were painful and slow. Whole districts lost heavily in population; others were forced to find new uses for the land. Unfortunately the structure of French landholdings and the traditional contracts between tenants and landlords were badly adapted to the new conditions, so tradition added its weight to the problems of change.

An ungracious Nature that failed to endow the land with coal cannot be held solely responsible for the failure of the nation to adjust itself to the economic civilization of the nineteenth and twentieth centuries. The traditional ideals of the French must bear their share of blame. Somehow the French bourgeoisie accepted the feudal code that branded trade and manufacturing as ignoble. One does not find this stated overtly, but the very fact that so many of the French entrepreneurs seem to have looked upon their business efforts as a means of providing the wealth necessary for retirement is indicative of a moral value. Sons of retired men did not regard the creation of great economic institutions as a suitable goal for their efforts; they became officials in the government, entered the professions, or joined the country gentry. Again, these values probably provide personal satisfactions, but they do not build industrial concentrations on the modern scale. On a lower level of aspiration, as André Siegfried has pointed out, the French penchant for the "little"—a little business, a little farm, even a little graft—has further limited the economic vision; France is a nation of small enterprises and, paradoxically, the *Petit Parisien* became its largest newspaper.

In another age these values would have created no serious difficulty, but in the century 1850–1950 they were out of line with the dominant trend in the world, and thereby had within them the seeds of disaster. The French themselves became acutely aware of the gap that was appearing between their economy and that of their more advanced neighbors when the World Fair at the opening of the twentieth century dramatically called attention to the technological and industrial developments elsewhere. Coming as it did after twenty-odd years of economic stagnation, this fair at Paris aroused considerable self-criticism. The nation became painfully aware of its declining birth rate, the flight from the land, and the relative backwardness of its industries. Clearly the same France that functioned so well in an age of wood, wind, and water was falling behind in an age of steam and iron. A glance at the files of any of the more thoughtful French periodicals in the first years of the twentieth century will reveal that this problem, even as much as the more inflammable Dreyfus Case, engaged the attention of thoughtful

Frenchmen. It was at this very time that the term *élan vital* came into currency; perhaps the French themselves understood the danger that was threatening the vital springs of the nation.

It is probably an unwarranted assumption that either economic institutions or economic values can fully explain the course of human behavior. It would be attractively simple to show that lack of coal and a limited aspiration are at the roots of the disorder in French society, but such an explanation would have to meet the objection that other societies in Europe where coal is also scarce and men's economic aspirations also limited have not followed the French pattern. Thus to escape the pitfalls of economic determinism we must look to other aspects of French life that also worked to the detriment of the *élan vital* of the nation.

The most important of these, I believe, is to be found in an understanding of the basic postulates of French society. As limiting to man as his economic environment are his postulates about the world. The things that men believe are the true limits of their vision, and these limits, in turn, circumscribe their development.

Bourbon France rested firmly upon a set of postulates that seemed to be drawn directly from the facts of French history. The idea that society was an organic unity, made somehow by God, was fundamental to all political action. The law was of divine origin; custom, tradition, and usage were regarded as sacred. Men no more assumed that they could give a constitution to society than that they could, to quote De Maistre, give weight or extension to mass. The *Honnête Homme* who provided the ideal for the society accepted his lot with a Christian fatalism that testified to his faith in God and his conviction that the world was a vale of tears through which men must pass to reach the kingdom of heaven. Such an idea might have caused a disassociation in society had it been the mirror for the nineteenth and twentieth centuries, but in the seventeenth and eighteenth it created no difficulties.

In the eighteenth century, however, there was an intellectual revolution that had great influence in the upper classes of society; in the following century it affected the whole of the nation. The revolution can best be described by its catchword: *L'esprit géométrique*. It was the same Cartesianism that had provided the guidepost for so many of the great minds whose scientific labors in the seventeenth century became the intellectual capital of the succeeding period. This *esprit géométrique,* generalized in the eighteenth century, became the very foundation of French thought. Fontenelle, its high priest, explained that any work—be it in science, philosophy, morals, or esthetics—would be better, all things being equal, if it were written by the hand of a geometer. It was an idea that easily sank into the French mind; the French language with its exact syntax and its controlled vocabulary undoubtedly facilitated its widespread acceptance.

The basic postulate of this Cartesian philosophy is a belief in a mechanical world that is subject to law. The assumption that the world of nature and of men is a machine was buttressed by a second postulate, namely, that if it worked properly, it would be friendly to man. The Creator was thus assumed to be benevolent. This mechanistic rationalism is really not dissimilar to the Thomistic or Aristotelian, except in that it rests on different postulates and does not assume teleological causation. Like Newton, who discovered the time-machine of the universe, the Cartesian philosopher failed to understand that the world has a history, and, therefore, that the key to many of its mysteries can be understood only in terms of process. If one assumes a static entity, a mechanistic organization, it is easy to believe that the evils of the world can be eradicated by adjusting the mechanism. This conception led to an inordinate confidence in the efficacy of constitutional form and reform. With a limited postulate, politicians and theorists erected little worlds within the greater one in hopes of creating a world more nearly suited to their needs.

Men have no difficulty in assuming that what they believe to be true is in fact true; this human failing made it possible for men to find that the aspirations and hopes of their own group were political absolutes that should forthwith be written into the laws of the land. Thus the law ceased to be a traditional thing written by God, by the wisdom of the race, or by the General Will, and the entailed inheritance of society became a political football, subject to the vicissitudes of election or revolution. As early as 1790 Burke warned the French of the evils inherent in their fulsome acceptance of the geometric conception of politics; and the history of the nineteenth century unhappily bore out his doleful predictions. When men can no longer agree upon their common tradition, belief in a mechanistic structure of society can easily create a pathological situation.

A second line of thought, also growing out of the thinking of the eighteenth century, added to the disorder when it was combined with Cartesian cosmology. This was the idea that morals, manners, and customs are relative. Between 1600 and 1800 travelers and philosophers pondered the fact that variations in values were determined by differences in culture, tradition, and geography. When applied to politics, this conception of moral relativism became individualism and liberalism; when liberalism is applied to a community, however, its members must not forget either Aristotle's insistence that man is a political animal and that man outside of society is less than an animal, or Bodin's sage counsel that there must be a "greatest good" in each society. In other words, differences in moral values can be tolerated as long as there is a core of unanimity that will hold the community together. Failure to understand this fact, as we in the United States are recognizing today when we legislate against certain Communistic activity, may end in disorder. In France this moral relativism has justified disregard for all traditions. Péguy, writing in 1910, lamented the breakdown of the community of the old France, the France of his youth that still had the core of French civilization and tradition; his belief that it was already destroyed was too harsh a judgment, but the process at work seemed to justify his pessimism.

It is with extreme reluctance that I reach the conclusion that the Enlightenment of the eighteenth century must share the responsibility for the disorders of the twentieth. The men of Voltaire's generation, labored honestly to free the human spirit from the tyranny of ignorance, prejudice, and fear. They are not to be blamed for their postulates any more than we can be blamed for our own. The disorder is not of their making, but rather the result of continued use of their ideas long after new evidence had undermined the postulates upon which those ideas rested. Bergson was undoubtedly right when he argued so vehemently against Cartesianism, and Jacques Maritain is probably right when he insists that France must find a new axis for her social life. Unless it is found, the disorder may well become progressively worse.

There is at least one further factor that deserves serious consideration in this discussion of the basic postulates of French society. French national feeling—that is, their conception of themselves and their role in Europe—came into bloom at a time when France was a leading political and military power on the Continent, and it requires but little insight to understand that the nineteenth and twentieth centuries have deeply injured the pride of a great people. Between 1815 and 1914, with the exception of a few years under Napoleon III, the basic treaty law of Europe assumed French weakness and defeat. Even limited understanding of the July Revolution, the rise of Louis Napoleon, and the popularity of leaders like Boulanger, will testify eloquently to the gap between reality and national aspiration. Furthermore, the victory of 1919 merely emphasized that gap. It was won by a coalition, and when the coalition no longer sustained it, the victory turned to gall and wormwood. Unlike Swedes, Danes, or Dutchmen, the French—from the little people in the country whose forefathers were at Austerlitz, Jena, and Friedland, to the old families in the chateaux who try to remember the white flag of Henry IV— were psychologically unprepared to recognize their nation as a second-rate power. On the morrow of the defeat of 1870, the French began to rebuild the army and the navy: the nation never questioned the wisdom of this action. From that time down to the catastrophe of 1940, in face of a relative decline in population and a marked inferiority in industrial strength, the French government, no matter what might be its political complexion, persisted in the program of competitive military preparations. Nor were French ambitions confined to Europe alone; the fleet and the colonial empire were both indicative of a bid for world as well as European power. The military retrenchments of the past few years might indicate that France is ready to acknowledge the implications of the terrible defeat of 1940 and the readjustments of power in the modern age, but speeches in the Chamber, articles in the press, and the opinions of men on the street all indicate that the French face reality frankly, but are not yet ready to accept freely the full consequences of their position in the world.

It is a tragedy when a great man loses his strength and his personality; it is a catastrophe when a nation loses its assurance. To me the tragic pathos of the French problem can be summed up in a remark made by my hostess in a Parisian pension in 1937 when she called my attention to the notice about the air-raid shelter for the neighborhood. "Over there (in Germany)," she said with a choke in her voice, "the shelters will be safe; ours will be faulty." She wanted to be proud of the nation for which her husband had given up his life in 1916; she wanted to believe in the community that had given her nurture, but she had lost faith and with it her nerve. These simple words are dramatic evidence of the failure of the *élan vital* of a great people.

II THE POLITICAL FACTOR

Pierre Laval

SPEECH AT A SECRET SESSION OF THE NATIONAL ASSEMBLY, VICHY, JULY 10, 1940

Pierre Laval (1883–1945) remains one of the mystery men of contemporary French history. A leading figure of the Third Republic during the interwar period, he was summarily tried, sentenced, and executed, in 1945, for his activities as head of government during the Vichy regime. Yet, to this day, many Frenchmen still think of Laval as a sincere patriot who simply cast his lot with the wrong side. Be that as it may, after the Armistice of June, 1940, he quickly came to the conclusion that the parliamentary system was responsible for his country's defeat, and he is here trying to browbeat his audience of deputies and senators into granting full powers to Marshal Pétain. A few hours later, the National Assembly complied meekly by a vote of 569 to 80.

The occasion demands that I speak to you with the utmost frankness. The greatest crime committed in our country for many a year was certainly to declare war without adequate military and diplomatic preparations. . . . You are aware as well that all too many Frenchmen did not know why they were fighting. . . . We are no longer a free people. Why? Because we made every mistake in the book. We did not miss a single one.

When I turned on the radio, in the evening, at my little village in the Auvergne, I was hurt to hear a lot of talk about democracy and very little about France. Someone threw down the gauntlet with reckless abandon! Someone threw down the gauntlet and we were defeated! I have said, and I maintain that one does not save France by leaving her soil. To have done so would have meant the utter destruction of everything that was still standing in the land. That is why the Government is determined to do everything in its power, come what may, to prevent the Nazification of France. Our task is to salvage what we can from the wreck. To do this under the most favorable possible circumstances, we must be given the necessary powers. . . .

From *Le Figaro*, February 29, 1952. Reprinted by permission of the publishers of *Le Figaro*. [Editor's translation.]

I do not intend to say very much about England. Whenever I meet with some of our compatriots, especially from the occupied regions, who have been out of contact with French news media, and whose sole means of information have been English radio stations, I find that they are quite worried. They invariably tell me: "Be careful! Do not talk too much about England." Rest assured, I can announce officially that we have no intention whatsoever of declaring war on England. I must hasten to add, however, that whenever it is in our power to do so, we shall return blow for blow. I might also take this opportunity to remind the populations of the occupied regions of the facts. They will then be able to draw their own conclusions. First, it is a fact that England dragged us into war. Second, once having led us into war, she did nothing to help us win it. Finally, how did England behave toward us after we had been mortally wounded? We thought we were her ally. Yet it is no exaggeration to say that she dismissed us like so many mercenaries.

Some have charged that the proposal the Government is about to bring before you amounts to a repudiation of the parliamentary regime. Let me say loud and clear that this is not so. The Government's proposal is much more than that. It is the repudiation, not only of the parliamentary regime, but of everything that was and can no longer be. . . . There was too little awareness in France, beyond a few official platitudes, that certain policies and formulas had to be avoided if the peace were to be preserved. Remember? It was permissible to call someone a thief, a crook, or a pimp. But the one irreparable insult, the insult of insults was to call someone a fascist. Ah yes! The fact is that antifascism was the starting point of all our domestic and foreign policies. . . .

France was overly fat and happy. She used and abused her freedom. And it is precisely because there was an excess of freedom in all fields of endeavor that we find ourselves in the present straits. It is also a fact—I say this sadly because a great calamity has befallen us—that the existing institutions cannot be allowed to survive a disaster of this magnitude. Without wishing to impassion the debate, let me remind you that too much freedom in our schools contributed to our demise. One word was proscribed in our schools, the word *"Patrie."* Take a look at our neighbors. Italy was once on the verge of anarchy. One could walk the streets only at the risk of being assaulted by a mob bent on seizing power. In Germany, defeat had brought on misery, and misery, in turn, had brought on chaos. Well, what did these two neighbors do? They restored the idea of the fatherland. They began by teaching their youth to love their country, and that one's country is the family, the past, the village where one was born. These are the values which the schoolteachers failed to instill in our children.

The Constitution we have in mind is not reactionary. Both the current state of affairs in France and the temperament of our people preclude a longing for, or return to the past. We must plan ahead for the future. We must give the working class something more than the right to vote. The workers must be able to enjoy tangible rights under the impartial supervision of the State. Both agricultural and industrial laborers will receive full recognition for the amount and quality of their work. There will be only one aristocracy, an aristocracy of the intelligence. The harshest words against capitalism are uttered under democratic regimes. Yet only democracy or demogogy provide fertile soil for the utmost development and proliferation of capitalism. That is a fact. Ponder my words, because I speak the truth. During the last four years, our governments were, electorally speaking, an expression of the popular will. Yet, I can state without fear of contradiction that the railroads, banks, and insurance companies never fared better. It is a fact that under an authoritarian regime, under a regime where the State has reasserted itself, all such private interests must necessarily bow before the supreme interests of the nation. This is precisely what we intend to do. We will not emulate those regimes and institutions which curtail or prevent the full flowering of true liberties.

Let me say, to avoid the possibility of any misunderstanding, that in virtue of the full powers you are about to grant Marshal Pétain, the role played by the Chambers will necessarily be reduced. But his Government reserves the right, and intends to enlist the help of regularly appointed parliamentary committees. . . . We have no intention to become the slavish imitators of any other country, because this would mean that we were no longer worthy to call ourselves Frenchmen, that we had lost all pride in our race. Do you know why, above all, we are bringing up this proposal for a new Constitution? It is to obtain for France, I will not say the best, but the least harmful possible peace terms. Bear this in mind when you come to the public session.

Philippe Pétain

SPEECH OF OCTOBER 11, 1940

The "Hero of Verdun" was condemned to death on August 15, 1945, for his conduct as chief of the French State during the years of German Occupation. His sentence was commuted to life imprisonment, and he died in detention at the Ile d'Yeu in 1951. Marshal Philippe Pétain (b. 1856) is thus, in a very real sense, an incarnation of the ups and downs, trials and tribulations, and agonies that have raked France in modern times. His name is still venerated by many of his compatriots, who are actively campaigning to rehabilitate his memory. The Pétainists argue that but for the Marshal's "sacrifice," France would have been left at the complete mercy of the Nazis from 1940 to 1944. Only one thing is certain, as the following selection shows quite clearly: Pétain was among those who would lay responsibility for France's defeat at the door of the Third Republic.

Frenchmen!

Four months ago, France suffered one of the most thorough defeats in her history. This defeat was caused by many factors, not all of which were of a technical nature. In truth, the disaster was simply the reflection, on a military plane, of the weaknesses and defects of the former regime. Many of you, however, as I well know, loved that regime. Because you exercised the right to vote every four years, you considered yourselves to be free citizens in a free State. I will thus surprise you by saying that, to an extent unparalleled in the history of France, the State was at the mercy of special interests during the past twenty years. It was taken over in various ways, successively and sometimes simultaneously, by coalitions of economic interests, and by teams of politicians and syndicalists falsely claiming to represent the working class.

From Philippe Pétain, *Quatre années au pouvoir* (Paris, 1949), pp. 59–61. [Editor's translation.]

The succeeding majorities represented the temporary ascendancy of one or the other of these two factions. The majority's sole concern was all too often to eliminate the minority. When these struggles led to an impasse, one resorted to yet another dupery: the formation of a so-called "Government of National Union." A coalition of divergent political opinions does not make for coherence; a reservoir of "good will" does not necessarily translate itself into "one will." These swings of the pendulum, this modern-day vassalage had far-reaching effect. Everything pointed to the impotence of a regime which repudiated its very principles by resorting to emergency decree powers in the face of every serious crisis. War and defeat merely hastened the coming of the political revolution toward which the country was eventually headed. Hindered by such domestic political considerations, the regime was, for the most part, incapable of formulating and implementing a foreign policy worthy of France. Inspired in turn by a paranoid nationalism or a doctrinaire pacifism, characterized by lack of understanding and weakness—at the very moment when our victory called upon us to be at once generous and strong, our foreign policy could only result in disaster. It took us approximately fifteen years to fall into the abyss to which it inexorably led.

One day in September 1939 without even daring to consult the Chambers, the Government declared war. This war was all but lost in advance. We had been equally incapable of avoiding or of preparing for it.

Today, we must rebuild France on a heap of ruins.

The new order can in no way whatsoever imply a return to the mistakes which have cost us so dearly. Nor should it take on the features of a kind of "moral order," or of a revenge for the events of 1936.

The new order cannot be a servile imitation of foreign experiments—though some of these experiments are not without sense and beauty. Each people, however, must conceive of a regime suitable to its temper and genius.

A new order is an absolute necessity for France. Our tragedy is that we shall have to carry in defeat the revolution which we were not even able to realize in victory, in peace, in an atmosphere of understanding among equal nations.

Charles Maurras
THE APOLOGIA OF AN INTEGRAL NATIONALIST

Charles Maurras (1868–1952), the prophet of Integral Nationalism, is emerging as one of the most influential figures of twentieth-century France. For some forty years, as the uncontested leader of the neo-monarchist, reactionary, ultra-nationalist, and anti-Semitic Action française *movement, he pursued a relentless "politics of hate" against the Third Republic. His writings place him among the most incisive critics of democracy. Maurras, who had opposed the war, wholeheartedly endorsed the Vichy regime and denounced with equal fervor both the Resistance and Gaullism. Immediately after the Liberation, he was tried and sentenced to life imprisonment for "intelligence with the enemy." In characteristic fashion, Maurras turned the trial into an interminable apologia pro vita sua, from which the passage below is taken. While the tone and flavor are unmistakably Maurrassian, the line of argumentation is quite representative of rightist opinion.*

Now, listen very carefully to what I am going to say. Listen to what the *Action française* was alone to point out at the time. It was in the fateful year of 1935, even as we were giving up the Saar, that the French democratic parties became the proponents of an offensive war.

So long as the occupation of Mainz and the Rhineland gave us the means of waging war from a commanding position, so long as we could easily invade Germany and we even controlled a portion of the German border from the Upper Saar salient, their Briands and would-be Briands shied away from the very idea of war as from a monstrous impiety. We then had all the elements of strength and victory in the palm of our hand, but we refused to take advantage of the situation. Yet, no sooner had we lost our strategic advantage, than we adopted a militant, aggressive, and dangerous attitude. It seemed as if some Frenchmen welcomed the idea of defeat. You bleated: Peace! Peace! when you were strong; you started screaming: War! War! the minute you became weak.

One of the *Action française*'s most ardent campaigns was thus

From Le procès de Charles Maurras: Compte rendu sténographique (Paris, 1946), pp. 78–93. [Editor's translation.] Reprinted by permission of Editions Albin Michel.

waged against these pacifists turned warmongers. They clamored for war against Italy as early as September 1935; against the Spanish Nationalists as early as July 1936; and against Germany as early as 1938 and 1939. The *Action française* fought a battle on three fronts for three full years. In the year 1936 alone the war party made tremendous progress. A whole segment of Parliament, the steering committee of the Republican *"pays légal,"* became converted. A hundred and forty Socialist, Radical-Socialist, and Christian-Democratic deputies signed a petition demanding sanctions against Italy. They might as well have petitioned for an immediate outbreak of hostilities.

And, while the country was thus following a one-way road to war, what do you think was the Government's first action in 1936? On February 13, the Sarraut Ministry ordered the dissolution of all the nationalist and patriotic Leagues because a group of the police's *agents provocateurs* had scratched Léon Blum's ear in a slight scuffle. What a wonderful way to kindle a fighting mood in the country! Here was a new and very original version of the *Union Sacrée* of World War I!

A month later, March 1936, the Germans reoccupied and remilitarized the Rhineland in violation of treaty agreements. M. Sarraut issued a few shrill threats. He might have acted, had he possessed the means. But what can one do without an army? Bargain? He bluffed! He screamed! Yet, like everybody else, he knew all the time that one does not declare war on the eve of general elections. Afterwards anything goes. But not before. The Legislative Assembly of 1792 had already been elected when it declared its great and long war. Napoleon III had already been endorsed by the May plebiscite when he declared war in July 1870. M. Blum himself toyed with bellicose ideas once he had obtained his majority. But neither he nor M. Sarraut had the guts to alienate the electorate by ordering serious military measures. The Germans moved in where they pleased, when they pleased. As in the case of Mainz and the Saar, we had simply lost another strategic position. I am not to blame because the whole world then drew its own conclusions as to the politics and strength of the Republic. As always, the Republic had behaved like a scatter-brained woman!

The next month, the elections of 1936 were held. The Oath sworn on July 14, by all the parties whose leadership included some accomplices in the great Stavisky swindle, was carried out. The Communists, Socialists, Radical-Socialists, and Christian-Democrats, went to the polls hand in hand. The result was a handsome majority, and an even more handsome Ministry, headed by an adventurer named Léon Blum. This was the same Blum, who had once told the French people: "I hate you." The havoc raised by that sterile revolution known as the Popular Front is common knowledge. Its capacity for destruction was surpassed only by its impotence.

Late in October 1936, I was sentenced to jail because I had tried to prevent our going to war against Italy—an old ally, who had only recently rendered us a great service at the Brenner Pass. The judgment was enforced without an hour's grace. I am not complaining, because the two hundred and fifty days I spent in jail earned me a Civic Crown, bestowed at *Magic-City* in the midst of a host of excessively generous Parisians.

My freedom once regained, I began an intensive campaign of articles, meetings, and conferences, in an attempt to warn France of the frightful prospects stemming from the incompatibility between a policy of senseless warmongering and our pitiful weakness. . . .

I tried to show how our military establishment had been systematically reduced by the Progressive Governments which came to power in 1924, and again in 1932. The Geneva clique had greeted them with shouts of: "The Left is coming to power! The Left is coming to power!" Well, the advent of the Left meant at once disarmament and France's drift toward war, in spite of her declining birth rate, her lack of adequate forces or a solid continental alliance! Although our whole army was organized on the concept of defensive war, our first task would be to come to the help of our allies of the Little Entente, whose prime qualifications were the depth and number of their quarrels and the eagerness with which they had loosened the ties that bound them to us! What could we possibly do for the Poles or the Czechs? Where were the shock troops needed to break through the Siegfried Line? The morale of the French people, undermined by bitter memories of the "War to end Wars," and the size of our population, reduced by the loss of two million men in four years, ruled out the possibility of demanding new bloodshed, new sacrifices from the nation in pursuit of chimeras. One simply failed to find a rationale for going to war.

One found it even more difficult to explain the transformation of pacifist sheep into bellicose lions. These questions which I raised from one end of France to the other were never answered by anyone. I might add that both the official and unofficial press, from *l'Ordre* to *l'Aube,* showered me with insults. Yet these lies and invectives were never followed by a direct answer to my question. You wanted peace while you had an adequate military establishment; you began clamoring for war after you had disarmed. Not one of their writers was able to explain why they had always refused to use the power they once held; or why they pushed us, rushed us into war once we had become powerless. Folly? Treason? History, one day, will provide us with an answer.

Ours was not the pacifism of sheep. We did show, however, that peace was an absolute necessity for France. An objective analysis of the situation had led us to the conclusion that French intervention was then out of the question. But since we entertained no illusions about Hitler and Germany, we also realized the need for precautionary measures.

Thus each and every one of our demonstrations was summed up in a single word printed three times in different type: *Armons!* Armons! *ARMONS!* And how did the parties of the Left react to these campaigns? They replied with propaganda leaflets complaining that the budgets of the Ministries of the Navy and Aviation were siphoning off funds which might have been more usefully spent on schools and hospitals. They even accused our poor governors of trying to curtail benefits, services, and the right to strike. In the meantime, young ministerial aides, like M. Marceau Pivert, were conducting furious campaigns against Civil Defense in the popular districts of Paris! All this with war in sight! As in 1914, the Socialists persisted in their disarmament campaigns!

Nevertheless, in September 1938, our sustained and energetic campaigns, backed by Parisian public opinion, resulted in a stand-off at Munich. The outcome of the crisis was all to the country's advantage, since we were then even less prepared than we would be in 1939. Soon thereafter, however, Daladier began to weaken. He must have come to the conclusion that war was inevitable while in his nightshirt. About that time, he personally intervened to cripple our rearmament campaign.

In July 1939, I returned from Algeria, full of forebodings about the situation on land, on the sea, and in the air. . . . I found Parisian opinion upset by the sad realization that we did not have enough planes. On this point, at least, everyone was agreed. "Well then," said I, "let us build some planes." I was told that it would take too long. When I proposed that we should buy some, I was told that we lacked the money. I then launched, on the front page of the *Action française,* the idea of assuring the freedom of French skies through a national subscription. Since we could only hope to raise a few millions by ourselves, I invited the other newspapers, regardless of political opinion, to join in our endeavor. We might thus have been able to raise the necessary billions in short order. Well, the very same Government which deemed war to be inevitable, which was in a much better position that we were to know the true extent of our inferiority in the air, used every means at its disposal to insure the rejection of my offer. Was it because of our royalist predilections? The national interest should have been given precedence over the spirit of party. In any event, it would have been an easy matter to pick up the idea through a member of the Republican press. We would certainly have joined in the campaign heartily.

I issued unheeded pleas throughout the first half of 1939. I had said and written on many occasions that Hitler was our Public Enemy Number One. "Well then, what are you complaining about," countered the warmongers. As if the mere identification of a Public Enemy means that one should immediately jump on him, without giving a moment's consideration to the time, place, and means of the attack! The events of 1940–1944 have since shown us that even such large, rich, and heavily populated powers as the United States and the British Empire needed many seasons to realize their potential. We saw them resist for long years Moscow's imperious demands for a Second Front *hic et nunc!* But this example is beyond the point. The most elementary common sense dictates that one does not go to war without first having prepared for it.

We would have been much better off to await the possibility of an attack with a stout heart. In such an eventuality, we would at least have gained a moral advantage from not being the aggressor. The mobilization order of 1914 was answered enthusiastically because we had been invaded. If need be, the peasants would have fought off the invader with their pitchforks. Every last soldier knew why he was going to the front. A few scattered, artificial demonstrations to the contrary, the mobilization of 1939 was carried out in acceptable if hardly edifying fashion, because the men did not know why or against whom they were marching. Hitler? The men in the barracks had never heard of him. We had not even allowed the publication of *Mein Kampf* in our country. Fascism? This was a dirty word to the squabbling politicians. But politicians do not serve at the front, and those who do the fighting are not politicians. Finally, a war to make the world safe for democracy had little or no appeal. Democracy was bankrupt throughout the land, and whatever it may have meant in London or Washington was unknown to the majority of Frenchmen.

Edouard Daladier

WHY FRANCE WENT TO WAR IN SEPTEMBER, 1939

Trained as a historian, Edouard Daladier (1884–1970) left the academic profession for a political career that was to involve him in some of the most controversial and crucial episodes of the latter-day history of the Third Republic. His endorsement as Prime Minister by the Chamber of Deputies on the night of the February 6, 1934 riots, gave rise to the legend of Daladier "le fusilleur," and he was to represent France at Munich, and eventually to lead his country into war during his next tenure at the Hôtel Matignon (1938–1940). Naturally enough, this earned Daladier a prominent place on the bench of the accused at the Riom trials. After the tide had turned once more, the former Premier was able to state his case under more favorable circumstances before the postwar Commission of Inquiry in 1947. The reader will want to weigh his testimony against the views expressed by Laval, Pétain, and Maurras.

From *Les Evénements survenus en France de 1933 à 1945, Témoignages et documents recueillis par la commission d'enquête parlementaire, Rapport—Annexes (Dépositions)* (Paris: Presses Universitaires de France, 1947), I, pp. 59–62. Reprinted by permission of the Secretary General of the National Assembly of France. [Editor's translation.]

Do not believe, as was charged during the years of occupation, that the French Government went to war recklessly. Do not believe that the decision for war was taken at the meeting of August 23 [1939].[1] This was no more than an advisory meeting. I have never been one to make use of scapegoats. I have always assumed full responsibility for my decisions. On that occasion, I simply wanted to have the frank and objective opinion of our military leaders. Since the Government alone was responsible to the nation for its decisions, it was not my custom to delegate policy-making powers.

For eight days, from August 23 to September 3, the Government left no stone unturned in a last attempt to save the peace.

It has been alleged that the type of army we possessed precluded the possibility of our giving effective help to Poland. Yet our military leaders pledged themselves, by the Franco-Polish Convention of July 4, 1939, to begin probing attacks within seventy-two hours of mobilization, and to launch an offensive seventeen days after mobilization. I note also that General Vuillemin declared, at meetings of the Permanent War Committee, as early as 1938 and again in 1939, that "even obsolescent bombers would be capable of carrying out night bombing missions over Germany." You will see that this was an important factor when we come to a discussion of the military operations.

Be that as it may, we did everything in our power to prevent the outbreak of hostilities, because we were under no illusions as to the nature and meaning of modern war. We worked night and day to find an acceptable compromise. We went as far as was humanly possible. Someone dared to write an article titled: "To Die for Danzig." In fact, it was never a question of dying, or even of risking the life of a single French soldier for Danzig. On the contrary, we held that Danzig was a city in which a very small Polish minority was lost in a mass of Germans. We were in constant touch with the Polish Government during the last days of August. We proposed, and it was agreed, that should the Danzig Senate vote to rally to the Reich, Poland would not consider this a *casus belli*. We never stopped trying.

---

[1] The reference is to a meeting of the Permanent Committee of National Defense. It was attended by the Prime Minister, the Ministers of the Army, Navy, and Air, and the Chiefs of Staff of the three branches of the armed forces. [Editor's note.]

But why give you a detailed account of these last-ditch efforts? I simply would like to dispel the widespread belief that the French Government plunged blindly into war. The French Government did not go to war blindly. It went to war with a heavy heart, with a full awareness of the devastation to come. The French Government knew that France was but the vanguard of a coalition army. It knew, other opinions to the contrary, that it would be a long war, that ruin would heap upon ruin, catastrophe upon catastrophe. And that is why the French Government did everything in its power to prevent the outbreak of hostilities.

When, on August 25, Hitler informed me through M. Coulondre, that he could not back down on his demands, I replied—the letter has been published—that, in the event of war, both the French and the Germans would doubtless fight with much courage, but that the ultimate result would be the ruin of Europe, and most probably the triumph of barbarism. The French Government explored every possibility. We urged Poland to accept Hitler's offer of direct negotiations. But when the Polish Ambassador, bowing to French and English pressure, called on Mr. von Ribbentrop, the latter delayed the audience from one p.m. to late in the day. Von Ribbentrop listened without saying a word. He did not reply to any of the Polish declarations and proposals. Yet some two hours later, he summoned the English and French Ambassadors. He read them, at an extremely rapid pace, a note containing the German demands, and added that since Poland had turned them down, there was no point in further negotiations.

This note, which was later broadcasted, had not been shown previously either to France or, more important, to Poland. What Poland turned down were not the demands of the von Ribbentrop note of August 31, but those contained in Hitler's note of the 29th. The latter had asked for Danzig and the Corridor, the whole of Pomerania, and parts of Silesia. He had also stipulated that no final territorial agreements concerning Poland could be reached without the concurrence of Russia.

Gentlemen, that is exactly what happened. And so France found herself at war. After the defeat, in an atmosphere of polemics and lies broadcasted by the official radio network, and during the long hours and nights of captivity, I often wondered whether I had not committed a grievous blunder by declaring war at that particular moment. Would I have been better advised to give in to Hitler's ultimatum, abandon Poland, and wait for a more opportune occasion? I know that this is the thesis defended by some—notably the Communists in October 1939. I will have more to say on that score at the next session.

I do believe, however, that, in spite of the tragic sequel, France had no alternative. Had she taken a different course, had she bowed before Hitler, France would not only have been dishonored, but she would have acted against her best interests. Again, in spite of what followed, I insist that we had no alternative. If we had not gone to war, France would have earned the contempt of the democratic world. Neither Great Britain nor the United States would ever again have been willing to sign the least pact with us. And, in the final analysis, we would not have avoided war. What would Hitler have done once he had gobbled up Poland's chief resources? These are only hypotheses. One does not rewrite history. But, if I may be allowed to speculate, what would Hitler have done? Would he have crushed Poland and gone on to attack Russia in the Spring of 1940? It is by no means certain that in the Spring of 1940, Russia would have been able to parry the first onslaught and turn the tide of battle as she did toward the end of 1941. The fortunes of war are subject for debate, but it is a fact that not a single country in the world was able to stop the German army at its borders. And, although Russia was saved by the courage of her soldiers, the tenacity of her people, and the strength of her industry, the fact remains that in the beginning she lost two thousand kilometers of her richest, most fertile, and most heavily industrialized territory to the German army.

Had Germany jumped on Russia in the Spring of 1940, can you imagine any French Government asking the French people to go to her help? After the Nazi-Soviet Pact? After the publication of the secret clauses of that Pact? One may hypothesize further that before he attacked Russia, Hitler would have demanded some guarantees from France. Are you so sure that there would not then have been a Government in Paris, ready to give him these guarantees in order to avoid war? These are good questions to ponder in one's solitude.

For my part, I believed then as I do now, and I shall try to get you to share this conviction, that France was initially capable of resisting, if not of invading and defeating Germany. I feared that we might well be pushed back in some areas of the front. But I did not for a moment envision the possibility of a military collapse. In my mind, this collapse was due less to deficiencies of a technical or material order, than to faulty military doctrines, and even more to the difference between the doctrines of the two armies, and to the tremendous strategic surprise which was sprung at the time.

I am not here to prosecute the military leaders. They prosecuted me at Riom, and that is reason enough for me not to want to do so. But if you study the campaign, you will see that the General Staff expected the German attack to come through Holland and Belgium. In 1914, we had expected the attack to come on the right bank of the Meuse. This time it was expected to come in Holland, in Northern Belgium, and on the left bank of the Meuse. That is why the largest and best equipped divisions of the French army were moved to the North. Two or three days later, it became apparent that the invasion of Holland and Belgium was only a diversionary maneuver.

On May 12, I went to the Château du Cateau, in Belgium, to ask the King of Belgium to place his army under French command. I travelled by car in broad daylight, and stopped in almost every town. I saw the French motorized units pass by. I saw French soldiers park their trucks, tanks, and armored cars at every crossroad and public square, and jump out, in violation of all regulations, to fraternize with the Belgian people. The sky was empty. I did not see a single German plane. . . .

A day before, General Prioux, who commanded what was known as the Cavalry Corps, had telephoned General Blanchard, Commander of the First Army, to report that the developments expected in Belgium had not materialized, and to recommend a retreat to the fortified positions on our Northern border. General Blanchard concurred and forwarded General Prioux's recommendation to General Billote with his endorsement. General Billote disagreed, and issued an order (it has been preserved for the record) for the completion of what was known as the Dyle Maneuver. That is to say, the concentration of the French army on a defensive line extending from Antwerp to Namur.

I saw General Blanchard on May 12, after my meeting with the King of Belgium. I stopped at Valenciennes, where his headquarters had been established. I asked him whether he was satisfied with a maneuver, which I felt was taking place under strange conditions. I asked him whether he had been hampered by enemy air action. He answered that he had not. I saw no more than four or five bomb craters at Valenciennes. The population was roaming in the streets, and there were no other signs of damage inflicted by the German air force.

I was then only Minister of War and National Defense, but I have always regretted that General Blanchard did not inform me of the message he had sent to General Billote the evening before. The absence of German squadrons over the area gave me a premonition that the General Staff might have fallen into a trap. But I never learned of General Prioux's recommendation. On May 12, and for a day or two longer, we might have been able to carry out an effective retreat. Unfortunately, the order to return to our border positions was not given by the High Command—by General Gamelin, I think— until May 15. As I will attempt to demonstrate later, it was then much too late.

The essence of the strategic surprise was that the bulk and the most powerful elements of the German army attacked not on the left bank of the Meuse, but on the right bank from Namur to Sedan, at the center of our line, and to the rear of the French forces that had been moved forward. The German documents now in our possession prove that the enemy attacked at that point because he knew full well that this was the weakest link on our line of defense.

I have always believed that had we not been caught by this strategic surprise, or better yet, had we followed the advice given by Generals Prioux and Blanchard on May 11, we would have avoided the ensuing disaster and collapse.

Paul Reynaud

THE PARLIAMENTARY SYSTEM FAILED TO FUNCTION

Paul Reynaud (1878–1966) belonged to that category of French statesmen who have managed to combine a political career with prolific writing. His Au Coeur de la mêlée: 1930–1945 *is aptly titled because, throughout a long career, the author seldom shied away from a fight. Like Winston Churchill, Reynaud was too much of a maverick and a Cassandra to accede to the top post until a deep crisis made him the inevitable man of the moment. But there the parallel ends because he became premier just in time to lead France through some of her darkest hours (March 19 to June 17, 1940). As one of the leading actors in the drama, Reynaud has had much to say since the Liberation, and his books of memoirs and commentary occupy an important place in the debate over the debacle of 1940. In the following selection he comes to the calculated conclusion that France was defeated because "the parliamentary system failed to function."*

"The regime led the country to ruin," said Marshal Pétain, in a radio address on April 4, 1943. Following his lead, the Vichy press invariably accused the parliamentary regime of having been responsible for the defeat.

Why then were we defeated? "Because we did not have enough arms or allies," said Pétain, in a broadcast from Bordeaux on the morrow of the debacle. True enough, but let us suppose for a minute that France had been ruled, between the wars, by an absolute monarchy; that Pétain had been King, Weygand High Constable, and Maurras the Court Historian. Would we have had a tank corps? We have already seen that Pétain did not even want a single armored division. Would we have had an attack air wing? We have already seen that he discounted the role of air power in battle. Would we have had a pact with Soviet Russia, the only alliance capable of saving us? We have seen that he had publicly taken a stand against such an alliance. Weygand's position has already been made quite clear. Maurras campaigned violently against the Russian alliance. On the question of armaments, the latter was content to proclaim to

From Paul Reynaud, *La France a sauvé l'Europe* (Paris, 1947), I, pp. 540–551. Reprinted by permission of Monsieur Paul Reynaud. [Editor's translation.]

the four winds: "We must give our military leaders what they want!"
The trouble was that they did not want anything!

In the debate over the responsibilities for the defeat, the rightful
place for the men of Vichy is at the bench of the accused.

What is the greatest complaint about the parliamentary regime,
as it operated in France before the war? Instability. Instability at the
Ministry of War? From December 1932 to May 1940, with the exception of an interlude of two years and four months, we had the same
Minister of War. Instability of Command? From 1917 to 1940, we had
only Pétain, Weygand, and Gamelin—three Commanders in Chief
in twenty-three years!

Did Parliament ever refuse to provide the necessary funds for
national defense, be it for fortifications or armaments? It always
granted all requests in full. Did Parliament refuse to lengthen the
period of compulsory military service? The Chambers doubled it on
the very day the request was made.

The truth is that we were defeated because, during the interwar
period, both the succeeding Governments and the Parliament failed
to fulfill their functions. Was this due to institutional weaknesses?
Or can we lay the blame at the door of the politicians? Can we blame
the framers of the Constitution of 1875 for not having inserted a
clause to the effect that when one is the weaker party, one seeks a
powerful ally? For not having specifically stated that once one has
chosen weak allies, one must maintain an army capable of attacking
their would-be aggressors? For not having stated that a country must
match its potential enemy's armored divisions and attack air wings?
For not having specified that the French economy cannot thrive when
French prices are much higher than world prices? Can anyone maintain that either the Governments or the Parliament fulfilled their
functions?

Let us first take a look at the Governments. I have already shown
that the three distinguishing characteristics of our military policy,
originally formulated by Marshal Pétain, were ignorance, cynicism,
and incoherence. This policy was endorsed by the succeeding Ministers of War. Yet the very essence of parliamentarism is the supremacy of the civilian branch over the military establishment. Indeed,
the same thing is true of other types of regimes. Louis XIV and
Hitler, both civilians, always insisted on that point.

In a debate over our inability, in twenty years, to fortify the path traditionally followed by the invaders of France, because our Ministers of War "adopted the views of the Marshal as a matter of principle," I had occasion to remark that the military policy of France should no more be left to the soldiers than our financial policy should be left to the Inspectors of Finance, or our foreign policy to the diplomats. Such questions must be settled by statesmen—with the help, of course, of the technicians. Let there be no mistake, this remark should not be construed as an indictment of the War Ministry. Its Staff Officers were intelligent and cultured men. They were in that great tradition of sacrifice and disinterestedness without which there never would have been a French army. We must never forget that its history is interwoven in the history of France, and that its glories like its sorrows are those of all Frenchmen. But it is hardly surprising that, in the officer corps, the respect due to the commanders should extend to the establishment itself. From this stems the intellectual rigidity which is one of the causes for our army's inability to remodel itself. Some, however, managed to avoid this pitfall. Colonel de Gaulle is a case in point. When young colonels disagree with old generals over the nature of the war of tomorrow, the chances are that the young colonels are right. But the colonels must stand at attention before the generals. Who but the Minister of War can settle such issues? He must not, however, cast himself in the role of the generals' business agent, act on their behalf at the Ministry of Finance and before parliamentary committees, or plead their case in the Chamber.

One might object that the minister lacks the competence to solve technical problems. At a certain level technical difficulties are of little import. To begin with, all matters on which the technicians are in agreement can be considered as settled. In other cases, one must study the problem, weigh the merits of the conflicting opinions, and reach a decision. Could any Minister of Finance, especially after the devaluation of the dollar, have afforded not to formulate his own monetary policy? Yet, with all its ramifications involving the economy, finances, and social peace, this area is much more complex than the military sphere. Moreover, as I have said, all great political decisions are based on common sense. Is the charge true that, after 1919, some of our Ministers of War chose to give in to Marshal

Pétain, to perpetuate his legend and to use it as a shield, and thus failed to fulfill the function of their office, which was to stand up to him at the risk of compromising their career? We cannot affirm this with any degree of certainty, although some of them may well have acted in this fashion subconsciously. By delegating entirely to our top soldiers the task of formulating and implementing our military policy, they deprived the country of a statesmanlike strategy. Our military policy was incoherent because it was never thought out on the highest possible plane.

It was a common saying that "the ministers come and go, but, thank heaven, the civil service is always there to govern the country." Doubtless, the permanent staffs were fully capable of handling routine matters. But whenever a serious problem cropped up—and there was never a lack of them, the civil servants naturally enough refused to compromise their career by overstepping their area of responsibility. Can anyone blame them? Policy-making decisions are the minister's province. Moreover, a statesman, familiar as he is with each and every facet of the national experience, can always approach important problems with a broader perspective than a civil servant. In effect, a minister is to a ministry what a horse is to a cart. When the horse fails to pull, the cart does not move. Before the war, our successive Ministers of Finance were able to implement the most radically different policies without any changes in the main body of civil servants.

The Parliament was also to blame, in that it sanctioned economic, diplomatic, and military policies that were equally incoherent. A Parliament should no more be a rubber stamp than a wrecker of ministries. Its essential task is to study, approve or disapprove, and supervise the implementation of the various programs brought before it by the Executive branch. This is an important and difficult role which demands more knowledge and hard work than the framing of an insidious amendment designed to assure the defeat of a bill and perhaps of the Government itself. This primary task simply was not performed.

What did Parliament do, in 1933, when Hitler came to power, *Mein Kampf* in hand? It voted the reduction of the French army's officer corps by one-sixth.

In 1934, on the morrow of February 6, the Chamber appointed a

Commission of Inquiry to find out whether any politicians, besides an obscure deputy named Bonnaure, had had any dealings with the crook Stavisky. This commission worked feverishly for months, and, in the end, did not uncover a thing. During this very period the Doumergue-Pétain Ministry issued the famous note proclaiming that "henceforth France will rely on her own resources to achieve national security." Now, here was a statement deserving the scrutiny of a Commission of Inquiry. How could France, with her population of 41 millions, stand up to a fanatical Germany, whose industry was twice as powerful, and whose youth was twice as numerous as her own? With what allies? With what type of armaments? And, in view of the lingering depression, with what financial resources? Did not such questions call for the forming of a special commission made up of members from the Committees of National Defense, Foreign Relations, and Finance? Is it not certain that, had such a commission labored with half the dedication shown by the Stavisky Commission, the incoherence of our military, foreign, and financial policies would have become apparent to every last citizen? The very survival of France was at stake. Was this not a matter as deserving of attention as the "Bayonne Pawnshop Scandal" and Stavisky's jewels?

Did the Chamber fulfill its function, in February 1937, when it recognized that Germany was bulging with tanks and planes while France had none?

Did the Chamber fulfill its function, in 1934, when it allowed the depression to deepen in France by refusing, against all advice, to align the franc with the depreciated currencies of other nations? And did not the Chamber cripple the buildup of our defenses by following financial policies that led directly to sit-down strikes, the electoral victory of the Popular Front, and a shortening of the work-week at the very moment that Germany was increasing hers?

Why could not the Armed Forces Committee of each Chamber have said to the successive Ministers of War:

> *You are raising a defensive army. You think in terms of concrete, continuous front, and firepower. Yet France is committed to come to the defense of Poland and Czechoslovakia in case of German aggression. How are you going to attack Germany with a defensive army? Should Belgium be attacked, our army will have to fight an open-field campaign. Such an eventuality is all the more likely, since the Maginot Line is but*

*another inducement for the Germans to take the traditional invasion path
to France which runs right through Belgium. How are you going to fight
such a campaign with a defensive army? Will the French army push its
concrete before it, as Malcolm's army, in* Macbeth, *carried the trees of
Birnam Forest?*

Could not these same parliamentary committees have told these
same ministers:

*Your policies are incomprehensible. You claim that you are raising a
defensive army, yet it is being equipped with too few antiaircraft guns,
antitank guns, and antitank mines to match the offensive weapons of our
potential enemy.*

And why did not the Aviation Committee of each Chamber tell the
Ministers of Air and National Defense:

*Your policies are incomprehensible. We are raising a defensive army
on land. This obviously calls for a defensive air force. Yet, you tell us
that you are concentrating on the building of heavy bombers. Suppose
that these are ready at the outbreak of war and that they begin to bomb
German cities. They may well kill a few hundred civilians, and even
destroy a few German factories. But do you think that this will in any
way hinder the main German war effort? Such mosquito bites on the neck
of the German bull will not even slow down his charge toward Paris. It
is elementary common sense that not a single panzer should reach Paris.
Rather than cumbersome machines designed for long-range, spectacular
bombing missions, what we need are dive bombers and fighter planes to
support land operations.*

All the National Defense Committees should have concluded in
unison: "The ministers must devise new doctrines or we will replace
the ministers."

Then, and only then, the parliamentary regime would have functioned. But it failed to function. The appeal of all this incoherence
was that it represented the path of least resistance. But it would
never have carried the day without the endorsement of the "Victor of
Verdun," whom the Republic canonized until he turned around and
strangled it. This surrender to the Marshal amounted to the quasi-
dissolution of Parliament.

The various organs created by law to assure our national security
remained as inoperative as the Government and the Parliament.

Between the wars, the Supreme Council of National Defense met once, to discuss the instructions to be given our delegates at the Geneva Disarmament Conference. It never met again after 1933.

We have already seen that Fabry refused the Soviets' offer of a military convention without consulting a single one of the competent councils. . . .

Neither the Supreme Council of National Defense, nor the Military High Commission, nor the Supreme War Council, met at the time of the German reoccupation of the Rhineland in March 1936. They did not meet either before or after Munich. We thus have no official record of the deliberations which took place at the time of these important events.

None of these councils met after the Hitler-Stalin Pact. A report was issued after an unofficial meeting held on August 23, 1939; but it was not even distributed to the interested parties. No wonder that Guy La Chambre, the Minister of Aviation, and Gamelin, the Commander in Chief, should later contest its accuracy.

The question whether or not to organize an armored corps was never brought before the Supreme War Council. It was not asked to work out 'the structure" of a typical armored division until October 16, 1936. In spite of the lessons of the Spanish Civil War, the Supreme War Council never met to demand the creation of an attack air wing. During the six-and-a-half years of the armaments race, its meetings were presided over by the War Minister only four times, and never by the President of the Republic. The Prime Minister did not attend a single meeting.

During the first eight months of the war, the War Committee, chaired *ex officio* by the President of the Republic, met once in September 1939 to consider matters of secondary importance; and once in March 1940 to discuss Churchill's proposal for the mining of rivers. It was not asked to pass on such important matters as the decision to send Allied troops into Belgium, or the Finnish and Norwegian operations. What is the sense of having institutions if they are constantly bypassed?

Moreover, both the Government and the Parliament had been reminded of their obligations in preparing for war. They had also been reminded of their responsibilities. On March 15, 1935, speaking before the Chamber, I tried to explain the extent of the revolution in

the art of war brought about by modern technology, and hence the
need for the creation of an armored corps. I also warned that we
could not trust the army to modernize itself:

> . . . The General Staff lacks imagination and favors easy solutions. Let
> us not shirk our responsibilities. The General Staff is no more than the
> instrument of the civilian branch, and that is how it should be. Whenever
> this is not the case, the fault is not the General Staff's, but that of men
> who do not know how to make themselves obeyed. . . . Today, ours is
> the responsibility.

. . . On January 26, 1937, I inquired in the Chamber whether we
were to organize an armored corps, now that we knew Germany had
one. I continued:

> We are equally responsible for all financial, diplomatic, and military
> decisions. Gentlemen, here are some specific recommendations. I advo-
> cate the creation of a new Ministry of National Defense, with a single
> General Staff for all three military establishments; and the appointment
> of a Chief of Staff, who will act as supreme commander of all French
> forces in time of war. I further believe that we must embark on a crash
> rearmament program. In planning this program, the Government should
> never forget that—as I have often warned from this very platform, there
> are two German workers for every French worker; and that, as Mr. Hitler
> himself has reminded us, German war industry has been working around
> the clock for the past three years. Finally, we must organize special
> motorized and armored units.

Daladier, then Minister of War and National Defense, replied to
my criticisms. He first reviewed his current program: the activation
of a third light motorized division, and extensive study and experimentation for the eventual formation of armored units. He then went
on:

> I am in complete accord with the High Command on all these essential
> matters. I would like to see the end of these irresponsible attacks against
> the High Command in Parliament. The High Command is just as eager
> as we are to equip the French army with the best and most modern
> weapons. And I would like to take this opportunity to congratulate and
> to thank the High Command publicly—especially General Gamelin, the
> responsible commander of our army.

This statement reassured the Chamber. The deputies conveniently forgot that Germany had an independent armored corps, and that they had just been told that we would not follow her example. The Chamber was to be much less satisfied in May 1940. France's misfortune was not that she was saddled with a Parliament, but that hers was not worthy of the name. . . . We were defeated because the parliamentary regime failed to function.

A. Rossi
THE COMMUNIST FIFTH COLUMN

A. Rossi is the nom de plume of Angelo Tasca (1892–1960), a man whose career was an unusual blend of political activism and scholarly writing. Born and raised in Piedmont, he received a Doctorate in Modern Philology from the University of Turin, before serving in the Italian Army during the First World War. A militant Communist, Tasca went underground after Mussolini's advent, but he was finally forced to leave for Moscow in 1926. The three years he spent there as a member of the Comintern's Central Committee proved disappointing, and he was a confirmed foe of all forms of totalitarianism by the time he settled down to many years of research and writing in France. Tasca's productive period, interrupted by his activities as a member of a Resistance group during the Occupation, has earned him a well-deserved reputation as an outstanding student of Italian Fascism and French Communism. Les Communistes français pendant la drôle de guerre, from which the following excerpt is taken, was to have been the first volume of a major study on the causes for the debacle of 1940.

Following the new line set by Moscow, the Communist Party took an open stand against the war. In October [1939], Dimitrov proclaimed that "a courageous and relentless struggle against the war is the only legitimate policy." "The task of the hour," he added, "is to mobilize the masses against the war, in order that it might be brought to a speedy end." This declaration put an end to the hesitations of the French Party leaders, who had been alerted by Moscow in mid-

From A. Rossi, *Les Communistes français pendant la drôle de guerre* (Paris, 1951), pp. 204–205; 206–208; 209–210; 348. Reprinted by permission of Editions d'Histoire et d'Art, J. & R. Wittmann. [Editor's translation.]

September. In the introduction of a pamphlet containing Dimitrov's article, they emphasized that the Secretary of the Comintern had clearly shown that it was the workers' duty to wage a fearless fight against the imperialist war. The Party took up the Dimitrov thesis on every possible occasion. Denunciation of the war was thus the theme of Communist interpellations in the Chamber, and the core of their argumentation at the trial of March–April. In its annual message of greetings to the Soviet Union, on the occasion of the anniversary of the October Revolution, the French Party promised to wage "a merciless fight" against the imperialist war. And it kept the pledge. The leaders frequently reminded the rank and file of its "solemn duty." In a tract, *Aux membres du P.C.F.,* Thorez and Duclos reported with obvious satisfaction, that, as a result of the Party's campaign, "propaganda against the war is reaching all segments of the working class, in factories, in the fields, and *even in the trenches.*"[1] In its February issue, *Peuple de France* urged "the formation of a united front of all workers, under the banner of the struggle against the imperialist war, against the Daladier Government, and for peace." In an article, published in March 1940, Maurice Thorez wrote: "The Communist Party holds high and firmly, the flag of the Communist International, *the banner of the revolutionary struggle against the imperialist war.*" The Party called for the rallying of all progressive forces against the reactionaries of France, *"to bring the war to an end, to make peace."* The organizing of this struggle was the purpose of every tract and paper disseminated by the Communists. The Party boasted that it was *alone* in its opposition to the war, and the leaders actually reminded the German authorities and the Vichy Government of the fact, when they attempted to gain their good will after the Armistice. . . .

The Party's efforts to win over the army were closely linked to its nationwide campaign. Since there was very little military activity in the overwhelming majority of sectors until May 10, 1940, the army did not live apart from the population at large. With the exception of the evacuated zone, there was daily contact between civilian and soldier in billeting areas. Moreover, the soldiers retained close ties

[1] All italics in this selection are the author's.

with their families and friends, whom they saw on frequent leaves. As a result of this continuing dialogue, this exchange of views, of impressions, of complaints, of information—or, as was often the case, of misinformation, the outlook at the front came to reflect that prevailing in rear areas. Thus the morale of the army was highly sensitive to the currents of French public opinion, and the Party hoped to derive much benefit from this situation.

It was perfectly logical that the Communists should spare no efforts in their attempts to undermine the morale of the army. After all, they had refused to join the Sacred Union and they continued to be the antiwar party. The common soldiers, be they at the front or in staging areas, were their prime target. They had to be reached through every possible avenue, by every possible means. To propagandize the armed forces became the number one task of every party stalwart. As Thorez declared in an interview, *"the Communists have a clear duty to perform among the soldiers."* The December instructions emphasized that all members in uniform should be made aware of "the Party's position in the struggle against the imperialist war." The recipients of the first number of the clandestine *Humanité* were urged to send their copy to "a friend in the armed forces." The editorial of a subsequent issue expressed the hope that, by passing from hand to hand, the paper would eventually bring the good word to the soldiers in the trenches.

The leaders were well aware that the effect of their campaign would be blunted and that they would lose their hold on the rank and file, should the soldiers ever become isolated by the wall of military discipline. Hence their constant reminder to the latter that, even though they wore uniforms, they remained free men, citizens, and members of the working class. Proclaimed *Peuple de France:* "Soldiers, remember that you are first and foremost workers, peasants, and laborers, whose interests are opposed to the goals of the men who are forcing you to fight." *"Soldier, never forget that under your uniform beats the heart of a worker!"* read the banner-head of *L'Humanité du Soldat,* May 1, 1940. Soldiers, workers, and peasants were urged to fraternize and to unite for peace. This end would be reached through the rallying of all proletarian forces around the Communist Party.

Naturally enough, the soldiers worried about their families. And since at least one member of nearly every family was then serving in the armed forces, the Communists used this unbreakable link between the front and the rear to foment a climate of common hostility to the war. Wives were urged to let their soldier-husbands know "what was really going on" back home. Soldiers were encouraged to demand that "their families be respected and provided for." By exploiting an inherently difficult situation, often compounded by the mistakes of the Government, the Party hoped to generate a feeling of widespread discontent "in factories, in the streets, among women waiting in long lines to buy oil or coffee, among soldiers' wives queuing to collect a meager allowance, among soldiers, who had become aware of 'what was really going on' and wanted PEACE."

. . . The industrial plants remained the Party's principal field of activity. For one thing, there were many connections between the army and the factories. Mobilized workers with special skills were often sent back to war plants on temporary assignments, thus creating a steady channel of communications between the factories and the front. The delivery of war materials provided another opportunity for contacts between soldiers and workers. The Communists occasionally used this means of sending bundles of tracts and newspapers to the front lines. For another thing, in spite of the mobilization and Government repression, the hard core of the most loyal and most active Party militants was still to be found in the factories. Above all, the industrial plant was the vital cog in the all-important matter of war production. To a very large extent, the outcome of the war was to be decided in the factories. Any Communist success in hampering production would have automatic repercussions at the front. The Communists thus held a trump card which they did not hesitate to use. The Finnish War, involving the USSR as it did, led to the first act of sabotage. The Party openly urged on the workers: *"Use all appropriate means, use your intelligence and technical knowledge, to prevent, delay, and sabotage the production of war material."*

What were the number and importance of these acts of sabotage? To what extent did they actually affect war production? Such questions are very difficult to answer. A decisive verdict cannot be reached until material in the archives of military tribunals, industrial concerns, relevant ministries, the High Command, and the Riom Trials has been made available. An accurate inventory may never be taken, for many acts of sabotage escaped the scrutiny of factory inspectors. They were not detected until the defective equipment was used in action, during the Battle of France, and the debacle ensued before Parliamentary Commissions could look into the matter. . . .

Any attempt to assess the effect of these acts of sabotage on the morale and efficiency of the French Army leads one to two seemingly contradictory conclusions. It is quite certain that the majority of workers were never involved. The production of defective material entailed the recruiting of highly selected militants, of specialists whose will and determination went far beyond the mere "griping" through which the average worker expressed his opposition to the war. One might thus be tempted to conclude that the scope of the campaign of sabotage was necessarily very limited. On the other hand, since war materials in general, and aircraft in particular, are extremely delicate instruments, any worker taught the intricacies of the art by a specialist could easily be turned into an effective saboteur. A single saboteur, at the right place on the assembly line, could do untold damage. It was revealed at Rambaud's trial that "in the beginning, the young worker sabotaged no more than two or three aircraft engines a day. However, at his elder brother's urging, he ended up by sabotaging around twenty engines a day."[2] At the time of his arrest, seventeen out of the twenty aircraft engines in the shop where he worked were found to be defective.

One thing is certain: all the available records of large- and medium-size industrial plants involved in war production report instances of sabotage. It is equally true that the effectiveness of the campaign of sabotage was limited only by the strong measures taken by management and the *Sûreté Nationale.* Draconian methods were sometimes employed. For instance, following the discovery of defective material at factories in Saint-Denis and Courbevoie, all known Communists and would-be Communists were sent back to the front.

[2] An eighteen-year-old member of the *Jeunesses Communistes,* Roger Rambaud was tried and executed for his sabotage activities. [Editor's note.]

It cannot be said that the army's morale improved as a result of this move, but sabotage in the factories involved ceased as if by magic. In large enterprises like Renault and Farman such thorough purges were impossible. In any event, the cleverest and most dedicated saboteurs always managed to escape detection. In these two enterprises, management prevailed upon patriotic technicians and engineers to accept assignments as foremen and common laborers to help ferret out saboteurs. In this fashion "technical incidents" were kept at a minimum.

. . . The Communist Party and its Youth Organizations willed and organized the sabotage of war production, beginning with the Finnish War and continuing throughout the Battle of France. To this end they used all available means. Their responsibilities, both on a moral and practical plane, have been clearly established. In all fairness, it should be pointed out, however, that Communist sabotage was but one of many reasons, and not even the most important, for the technical inferiority of the French Army. This problem, or to follow another line of thought, the question of the misuse of what equipment was available, will not be resolved until much more documentation has been released to research scholars. The Riom trials tackled the problem without coming anywhere near to a solution. An impartial verdict is probably still beyond the realm of possibilities.

Without wishing to anticipate the conclusions of future historians, we beg leave to advance a few of our own, based on the careful study of available evidence. The harmful influence of the Communist Party on France's war effort extended far beyond its sabotage activities. This influence spread throughout the land as a result of the Party's sustained antiwar campaign. The feeling of solidarity between civilian workers and those of their brethren who were working at their side in uniform was skilfully exploited. By slowing down production, one and all hoped to keep the number of those who would be sent back to the front to a strict minimum. The Party also capitalized on the general discontent generated by the social policies of a rather shortsighted Government. Finally, the Party set out to make the war as "unpopular" as possible. It justified its most extreme policies and tactics with the slogan: *"An hour lost for war production is an hour gained for the revolution."*

. . . French Communists have often argued that the way to the debacle had been paved by a Fifth Column. This convenient explanation is much too superficial. The catastrophe of May–June 1940 was the result of a long political, military, and social crisis that had been worsening ever since 1934. But to the extent that the "Fifth Column" thesis has any validity, one must point out that from September 1939 to June 1940 the French Communist Party was its most prominent and active wing.

III THE MILITARY AND DIPLOMATIC FACTORS

Colonel A. Goutard

THE WAR OF MISSED OPPORTUNITIES

*Colonel A. Goutard's career as a professional soldier was in the finest tra-
dition of the French military service. Born in 1893, he fought in both world
wars, joined the Free French Forces after the fall of France, participated in
the Tunisian, Italian, and Liberation campaigns, and retired in 1948 with a
fair share of wounds and decorations. His interest in military history dates
back to 1926, when he served a tour of duty on the teaching staff at Saint-
Cyr. Whether or not one agrees with Colonel Goutard that the French had
a real chance to turn back the Germans in the spring of 1940 (the original
title of his book was 1940: La Guerre des occasions perdues), the excerpts
below give convincing support to his claim that the contending forces were
almost evenly matched.*

What happened in 1940? What was the cause of the collapse which
cancelled out a victory which had cost the French nation so much
blood, the blood of 1,500,000 who had fallen in vain? Only twenty
years after their sacrifice, France was completely invaded and
brought under the heel of those who had been vanquished in 1918.

The French people have only seen the hideous spectacle of disaster, and have been told that the tragedy was predestined, logical,
inevitable, and that no one was responsible unless it were the country as a whole.

On this sad 1940 campaign we have only, in fact, the memoirs of
defeated generals: the successive commanders-in-chief, the Chief
of Staff of the Northeast Front, army and corps commanders, and
lesser generals. But these commanders were not able to foresee
the coming of the "lightning war" based on the use of tanks and
airplanes; they had neither mastered it nor could adapt themselves
to it. How should they now be able to raise themselves above their
defeat and recognize its causes? Their writings are, in general, special pleadings *pro domo*, even though the writers have often, in-
voluntarily, criticized themselves.

They claimed that the French defeat was not a military one and

From Colonel A. Goutard, *The Battle of France, 1940,* tr. Captain A. R. P. Burgess
(New York, 1959), pp. 13–16, 23–44. Reprinted by permission of Ives Washburn, Inc.

that the army leaders could not be held responsible. They preferred to find metaphysical causes for it. They saw in it a kind of punishment from above. "It was caused," declared Marshal Pétain in his message of June 25, 1940, "by our moral laxness and our pleasure-seeking." Doubtless that is a part of the truth; but it was not the nation's "pleasure-seeking" which forced the Command to cling to a doctrine which was out of date, to work out an erroneous plan of campaign, to adopt faulty general dispositions, and finally to allow itself to be constantly outmaneuvered by the enemy without attempting the least counter-stroke. And all this at a time when the chance of victory was actually there!

Some have also tried to excuse the defeat by saying that we were overwhelmed by sheer weight of numbers and by weapons considerably superior to our own. As Pétain declared: "When battle was joined, all we had to set against this superiority were words of encouragement and hope."

But what do we know of those enemy forces? One of the most curious features of the memoirs of our generals, and of the official historical accounts and their slavish followers, is the complete ignorance in which they leave us of the true moral and material facts of the German Army of 1939 and 1940. Because this army conquered us, they represented it as a terrible and invincible machine.

In every war a certain number of clichés spring up based on impressions of the time, which offer a facile explanation of events, and which also pander to national sentiment and the self-esteem of its great national leaders. But with the passage of time and as it becomes possible to study what went on "on the other side of the hill," where the situation was often very different from what we imagined, we see clearly how mistaken were the popular beliefs which we then accepted unquestioningly.

We shall see, then, what were the facts about this all-powerful German Army which plunged into battle in 1939; its unshakeable morale, its long preparation for war; the invincibility of the Luftwaffe and the Panzers; the unassailable Siegfried Line and the extraordinary output of the German war industries. In speaking about the bluff of the *Wehrmacht* during the whole of the period between 1936 and 1940, we will certainly shock those for whom Stukas and Panzers bring up terrible visions and who give credence to well-worn clichés. But the facts and figures are there, and we also have the unanimous testimony of the German generals. The fact that Hitler won the trick does not mean that he held all the trumps. We had some, too, and they were more or less as good as his; but we should have known how to use them and cast them boldly into the game.

Our great leaders were deceived by a bluff which started as early as 1936, and had little confidence in their own army, which they had not been able to turn into a really battle-worthy machine. They had even less confidence in themselves, and suspected that their cut-and-dried traditional ideas were outmoded. They clung, nevertheless, to a doctrine and military procedure derived from the 1914–1918 war, and found themselves condemned to timidity of action and a completely passive outlook. As soon as they were faced with new tactics and an unexpected move, very different from that of the First World War, they could only resign themselves to a "Fate" which they deemed inescapable and to a "Destiny" they considered predetermined.

And even the nation, deceived by these oracles, accepted the defeat as wholly natural! It is high time, then, if only to provide a lesson for the future, that these facile and soothing judgments be revised.

"If the French Army has succumbed," wrote General Albord, "it was because our military thinking between 1919 and 1939 underwent a total eclipse without parallel." As this eclipse resulted in a doctrine of paralysis which left us prone to defeat, the blame has been placed on the government for committing us to a defensive war. We must not confuse the conduct of the war, which is the realm of the government, with the conduct of operations, which is that of the military command. Our great leaders did not need anyone else to tell them what strategy and tactics to apply. They themselves drew their "conclusions" from the 1914–1918 war. All their writings and teachings show this.

After the politicians, who are unquestionably partly responsible, many have blamed our soldiers. Péguy writes: "When we refuse to incriminate the leading characters for the part they played in events, we try to transfer the responsibility to the soldiers who played an insignificant part and the inert masses." Admittedly some of our troops were surprised and did fail in their duty. But they had been ill-prepared and badly employed. Not a word can be said against our troops in Belgium, on the Somme, the Aisne, the Maginot Line, the Alps, etc., and our tanks and air crews were as good as the Germans'.

As for the opportunities of victory, the existence of which has been denied because they were not taken, these really did exist. An opportunity is created, not by the will to use it but by the strategic or technical situation which presents it. We were too unprepared to seize these opportunities, and our will failed us, so they remained lost. . . .

Let us now take brief stock of the armies as they faced each other on May 10, 1940.

Manpower

Comparable effective strengths. On mobilization, the Germans had produced a *Feldheer* (field army) of 2,758,000 men, including pioneers, and had in the interior only 996,000 men. They had a total of only 1,800,000 trained men at their disposal (including regulars and reservists).

As for us, our mobilized army contained 2,776,000 men in front-line units, and 2,224,000 in the interior, not counting the special classes retained in industry. Moreover, all our reservists had completed either a year, eighteen months', or two years' service.

We must admit, therefore, that initially, even without counting British support, we had at least a numerical equality with the Germans, and that the advantage in training was on our side, whatever length of time had elapsed since training.

Furthermore, we had in 1939, on the eve of the war, 39,000 officers on the active list or actively employed, and 90,000 on the reserve. "All in all," wrote General Gamelin, "our officer corps was markedly superior, as it had been established a long time, whereas the German one was of recent standing." Unfortunately, this superiority had disappeared by May 10, 1940.

Comparable major formations. The German Army at first consisted of 52 active divisions, and at mobilization it could number

103 divisions: 89 infantry, 5 armored and 4 light, 1 cavalry and 4 motorized divisions.

On our side, starting off with 45 active divisions, we had 99 divisions: 81 infantry, 2 light mechanized, 3 cavalry divisions, and the equivalent of 13 garrison or fortified sector divisions, plus 7 cavalry brigades and 2 armoured brigades. Admittedly 10 of our divisions were in North Africa and 9 on the Alps, but the Germans had some 60 divisions massed in the East.

On May 10, 1940, of the *Feldheer*'s 147 divisions, 135 were on the Western Front (consisting of 118 infantry, 4 motorized, 10 armored, 1 cavalry, and 2 motorized S.S. divisions). As for us, out of the 115 divisions which we then had, 94 were on the Northeast Front or in the rear of this front (of which 70 were infantry divisions, 3 armored divisions, 3 light-mechanized divisions, 5 cavalry divisions, and the equivalent of 13 garrison divisions). We must not forget the 10 British divisions, which must be added to our 94. We therefore had 104 Allied divisions for the May battle against 135 German divisions in the West. Gamelin quotes the figure as 108 and General Roton as 105. There was, then, approximation in major formations, especially if one included the 22 Belgian divisions which were integrated into the Allied army at the beginning of the battle and which brought us from May 10 to 28 a degree of assistance not generally recognized.

On mobilization, the strengths of the opposing divisions were nearly equal. Our active divisions and our divisions of the "A" series were generally in good shape, but those of the "B" series, deprived of the active element, were very mediocre, and were quite incapable of taking part in a campaign before further training.

On the German side we know that the situation was more or less the same, as only the 52 active divisions were in a good enough condition to take part in offensive operations immediately. The 14 *Ersatz* divisions could take part after a certain delay, but the 35 reserve and *Landwehr* divisions were very far from being able to do so.

It seems, then, that even here there was a certain equilibrium between the French and the Germans in September 1939, but the balance had swung against us by May 1940. This was caused by the different uses made by the opposing armies of the unforeseen interval of eight months before real operations.

Armor

The excuse. Gamelin wrote in his book: "The argument put forward by the Vichy government, which has so profoundly befogged French opinion, was that in May 1940 the Germans had a crushing superiority in tanks."

The argument put forward to excuse our defeat was that our tanks were old and out of date and were also very heavily outnumbered by enemy tanks. General Doumenc, who was Chief of Staff at that time, wrote: "As the Treaty of Versailles only disarmed the defeated side, our army had carefully preserved the guns and the tanks to which it owed the victory. . . . We took great care to keep in good repair all our 1918 tanks, but the very existence of prototypes, fruits of much research, showed how antiquated were our resources."

This would seem to imply that in 1939 we had only our old 1918 Renault F.T. tanks, and merely a few modern machines for test and trial purposes. This was far from being the case, and in the figures which follow these vintage models will not be counted at all. But first let us look into the alleged crushing numerical superiority of the Panzers.

Extravagant estimates. The Information Bulletin of the *Deuxième Bureau* of May 10, 1940, estimated some 7,000 or 7,500 German tanks. When on May 15 M. Daladier expressed his astonishment at these figures, considering the great increase over previous estimates, Gamelin said to him: "This Bulletin is what one might call a 'smoke-screen' in case things turn out badly!" And as things turned out very badly indeed, a great deal of use has been made of this smoke-screen!

As one might well suppose, looking at German records now available to us, we can forget this estimate of 7,000 tanks. But we find it again in General Gauché's "Comparative table of strengths of the opposing armies on May 10" to be found in his book published in 1953 with the following comment:

> *There has been much discussion over this figure of 7,000 tanks, and some have thought it excessive. It has been admitted that this estimate was made on the assumption that each German armored division had as many as 400 tanks. But a tendency arose to reduce this establishment,*

especially during the campaign in Russia, in order to provide greater mobility and flexibility. Thus the number of armored divisions was increased without changing the total number of tanks.

In reality, it was not so much a question in Russia of obtaining greater flexibility, which did not need improving, but of satisfying Hitler, who was always insisting on more armored divisions when there were no tanks to equip them! They were forced, therefore, to redistribute existing tanks. It was in this manner that in 1942 the strength was made up to 31 armored divisions, consisting in most cases of only 2 battalions, and 10 of those divisions had only one! As Eddy Bauer wrote: "Hitler hoped to hoodwink his enemies and his country with these fantastic figures. He ended up by hoodwinking himself!" Furthermore, our *Deuxième Bureau* of 1940 quoted not 10 divisions of 400 tanks but 12 to 14 divisions of 500 tanks.

There again the misrepresentation was intentional. Gamelin wrote: "When the *Deuxième Bureau* submitted this figure of 500 tanks per Panzer division to me before publication, I passed it, thinking it might shake French public opinion and so alert them."

Actual number of German tanks. We read in Guderian's memoirs that on May 10 the 10 Panzer divisions had theoretically 2,800 tanks, but in reality only 2,200. In 1946, before the appearance of his book, he spoke to Major Rogé, of the French Historical Service, of 2,680 tanks. And elsewhere, a document produced by the General Inspectorate of Panzer Units, dated 1944, gave the figure on May 10, 1940, as 2,574 tanks. . . .

The number of French tanks. By May 1940 our factories had turned out 3,438 modern tanks, of which a certain number were in the interior or had been sent overseas. But so far as the battle is concerned, we are interested in those on the Northeast Front. According to Gamelin, this number on May 10 was 2,283 formed into 51 battalions: 12 in the three armored divisions, the equivalent of 12 in three light-mechanized divisions, and 27 as independent battalions. Each battalion had 45 medium or light, or 33 heavy tanks. To this we must add the 4th Armored Division, which arrived from the interior on May 16, equipped with 3 new heavy battalions of about 100 B-tanks (its light battalions had been sent to front-line units). This brings the total of our tanks in the battle area to somewhere in the region of 2,400 formed into 54 battalions—without mentioning the 600 old Renault tanks employed in protecting airfields. Roton, Chief of Staff of the Northeast Front, gives even higher figures. . . .

We must have had between 2,400 and 3,000 modern tanks, and if one adds those of the B.E.F., the total for the Allies would certainly be in the region of 3,000 as against the German total of 2,700 on their Western Front. One can scarcely talk about "the overwhelming numerical superiority" of the Panzers. But were theirs superior in quality?

The quality of the German tanks. To judge the effectiveness of a tank one must consider its armor, its fire-power, its speed, its range of action, and even its wireless equipment. Any one type is a compromise between these conflicting requirements. According to the employment foreseen for it, one is either forced to sacrifice speed and range of action for the sake of armor and fire-power, or else to use more of its space for increased horse-power and larger petrol tanks. With this in mind, were our tanks "better" or "worse" than theirs? Surely it all depends on the use to which they were going to be put.

As we were preparing only for a static war, in which tanks would be used as a supporting arm for the infantry by helping it across obstacles and concentrations of fire, it was imperative that they should have very thick armor. This made them very heavy. Speed and a wide radius of action were minor considerations in a slow, limited advance, from objective to objective, at a speed dictated by the other arms. The long pauses in the advance would permit frequent refuelling, and a long-range wireless-set was not really necessary, as the tanks would be within sight of each other.

The Germans, on the other hand, almost wilfully perverse, were planning a lightning war, with fronts breached by surprise attacks and immediate and deep exploitation. Large, independent armored formations would then lead the way into open country. Their tanks therefore required speed and a long range of action more than anything else. Thickness of armor was of secondary importance.

Unfortunately, it was the Germans who imposed their type of warfare on us, and not the reverse! Lacking speed and wide radius of action, our tanks either arrived too late or not at all, or ran out of fuel in the middle of the battle and had to be destroyed by their crews. In this respect, they were inferior to the German tanks. Our leaders deplored these defects as if they were fatal! And yet our tanks were like this because our leaders had designed them so. It would have cost them no more to have had them otherwise.

Although our tanks were inferior to the Panzers in mobile warfare, they should have dominated the battlefield as soon as they met them face to face. But they had to be there in sufficient numbers, at the right time and the right place. The refuelling would have to be organized to the last detail.

Comparative characteristics. Whereas all our modern tanks had protective armor 40 mm thick, the Panzer Kw I had no more than 8 to 13 mm, the Kw II had 12 to 14 mm, and the Kw III had 30 mm, all could be pierced by our modern tank and anti-tank guns. The Panzer Kw IV, weighing 20 tons, was no better protected, with a thickness of 20 mm, except for the 30-mm front plate.

As for their armament, a certain number of our light tanks had to be armed with old 1918 37-mm guns, with low muzzle velocity and therefore low penetration, either because they were ordered too late or because of delays in manufacture. But in general, our H-39 and R-40 tanks had a good 37-mm gun, and our medium D-tanks and fast Somuas had an excellent 47-mm gun. These two guns could pierce any enemy tank. As for our heavy B-tank, this was held to be the best tank in the world. It weighed 30 to 35 tons, it had an armor 40 to 70 mm thick—proof against all German guns—and a gun of 47 mm mounted in a turret and another of 77 mm in the body.

On the German side, a quarter of their tanks, on May 10, had no gun at all (Kw I, which had only two machine-guns), a good quarter more (Kw II) had only a small 20-mm gun; the others had one of 37 mm, and the Kw IV one of 75 mm.

But when it came to speed and radius of action, the German tanks, with their cruising speed of 30 m.p.h., were greatly superior to ours.

"In the main," to quote Gamelin, "one can say that in May 1940 the French units were better equipped to deal with German tanks than the German units were with ours." Be that as it may, the Germans themselves did not feel that their armor was in any way superior. Walter Goerlitz spoke of French tanks as being "more numerous, better constructed, and with far better armor protection than the German ones." How is it, then, that our tanks did not play the part on the battlefield that was expected of them?

Inferior organization of our armor. It seems that the fundamental reason for the ineffectiveness of our armor was a mistake in organization, caused by wrong military thinking.

The first anomaly was that whereas German armored units belonged to a separate arm, the *Panzerwaffe,* our own were under two different commands. Some were under the Cavalry Command (1,500 armored vehicles, of which 700 to 800 were tanks) and the rest under the Infantry Command (1,500 to 1,700 tanks). Consequently there arose two mentalities, two sets of instructions, and two aims.

Furthermore, the German armored battalions were formed into divisions, and the 10 divisions they had in 1940 were themselves grouped into armored corps capable of forming an extremely strong assault force or reserve, with their long range and their deep penetration tactics. More than half of ours, on the other hand, were dispersed as independent battalions, and used as a general reserve, destined to be distributed "in penny packets" to large formations, either *a priori* or according to the demands of the moment. We also had 3 armored divisions, formed only at the beginning of 1940. But an armored division is not made up of armored battalions only, and all the rest—motorized infantry, self-propelled artillery, signals, etc. —had to be improvised as best they could. In the event, these tardily constituted divisions were incapable of existing and fighting independently, and had to be linked with other major formations, i.e., welded into the general dispositions.

Admittedly, we also had 3 light-mechanized divisions formed into a cavalry corps, but these units could not fulfill the usual functions of armored divisions. In any case, the armored elements in them were soon dispersed!

The difference in effectiveness, considering that there were the same number of tanks on both sides, could not but be enormous. Against our dispersion, the Germans had concentration; against our attenuated line, they had an organization in depth. In the fury of the storm our independent battalions disappeared completely, and our armored divisions melted one after the other like snow in midsummer sun, without having any appreciable effect on the course of the battle.

This question of organization is of primary importance. A German author, von Weitershausen, wrote: "The integration and command system in the German armored divisions enabled them to play a decisive part in the first years of the war, even though they were numerically inferior both in France and in Russia. It was not until the enemy, and the Russians were the first, began in their turn to form large armored and motorized formations, capable of acting completely independently on a strategic plan, that a certain equilibrium was set up in the conduct of operations."

The Air

Even if many people admit that there were approximately the same number of German and French tanks, they will certainly not admit that this was so in the matter of aircraft. Vuillemin wrote: "Our air force ran into an enemy which outnumbered it by five to one." And surely the whole world was witness to the fact that our skies in 1940 were "void of Allied planes?"

This must be examined more closely. One thing alone is beyond doubt: the ineffectiveness of our air force in battle. But the question is: was this ineffectiveness caused by overwhelming enemy numbers, or an inferiority in the quality of our planes, or incompetence in our pilots? Let us look into these three points.

Number of German planes. According to statements by the Luftwaffe generals Meister and Kreipe, collected in 1947 by Colonel de Cossé-Brissac, the Germans had 3,000 planes at their disposal on May 10: 700 to 800 fighters, 1,200 bombers, 400 Stukas, 200 mediums, and 450 scout planes.

In the book which he published in 1956, Jacobsen, the German historian, gives these figures: 1,016 fighters, 248 medium bombers, 1,120 bombers, 342 Stukas and 500 scout planes, a total of 3,226 aircraft. This appears to have been the true strength of the Luftwaffe in May 1940.

Number of Allied planes. A document sent by the French Air Headquarters at the beginning of May 1940 forecast that on May 15 there would be 1,300 French aircraft "engaged or ready for engagement at the front," consisting of 764 fighters, 143 bombers, and 396 scout planes.

General Vuillemin submitted a document during the 1942 Riom trial according to which the French Air Force in May 1942 numbered 1,120 modern aircraft, of which 700 were fighters, 140 bombers and 380 were scout planes.

These data are more or less confirmed by the very detailed picture provided by Colonel Lesquen from air force documents. Lesquen gives the following figures for aircraft at our disposal in units or on call to the army: 700 fighters—i.e. single-seaters (Morane, Bloch, and Dewoitine) and 100 larger aircraft (Potez 63); 150 to 175 bombers: of which about 60 were Leo 45s; 350 to 400 scout planes: Potez 63s and some Bloch. This makes a total of 1,200 to 1,275 aircraft. Colonel de Cossé-Brissac speaks of 1,279 planes, of which 743 were fighters, 144 bombers, and 392 scout planes.

Admittedly, during operations this total is subject to a reduction— up to 33 percent—of grounded aircraft, which might reduce the fighter strength, for example, to 450 or 500. But as this would be the same for the Germans, we need not take this factor into account.

We also had 314 aircraft in other theatres, and 1,450 in the interior, under repair, awaiting equipment, in the training schools and under test.

But let us only consider the 1,200 aircraft serving with the army. With its 3,200 planes, the Luftwaffe therefore had a superiority of nearly 3 to 1. This was very much reduced initially by the partial intervention of the R.A.F. operating from bases in Britain and France. The British contribution was, however, very variable. General Vuillemin estimates it at 630 planes, of which 130 were fighters based in France on May 10. But if the Allied bomber strength was very inferior to its German counterpart, the fighter strengths on both sides were about equal, and this was the arm which swept the skies over the battlefield. Naturally, after May 20, in the face of the Panzers' invasion of northern France, the British squadrons returned to the British Isles.

Reserving itself from then on for the defense of Britain, the R.A.F. only intervened in France once more, brilliantly at Dunkirk. What would have happened if the R.A.F. had engaged the Luftwaffe from the outset and fought it out to the end? It is quite possible that with our assistance, it would have won the decisive victory it had to win by itself a few months later. This would have broken up the Panzer-Luftwaffe partnership and would have prevented the subsequent attack on Britain.

The quality of the Luftwaffe. German fighters were faster than ours. Whilst our Potez 63 and our Morane could do 300 m.p.h., and the Curtiss 306 m.p.h., the German Me 109 could reach 356 m.p.h. and the Me 110 (which was not very maneuverable) could do as much as 365 m.p.h. Their armament was more or less comparable with ours, except that our Potez had two cannons, whereas the German fighters had only one.

The British fighters were the Hurricane (309 m.p.h.) and the Spitfire (356 m.p.h.). The latter were based in Britain, but they wrought havoc on the Luftwaffe at Dunkirk.

But if the enemy aircraft were better than ours, our inferiority was to some extent compensated by the superior quality of our pilots, with their longer training. In any case, their better aircraft did not prevent our airmen from destroying three times as many of their aircraft as they did ours. In his *Bilan de la Bataille aérienne,* Vuillemin gives the following figures: 778 enemy planes shot down by our fighters and 240 by our anti-aircraft guns, as against 306 French planes shot down and 229 destroyed on the ground.

Was the sky empty of Allied planes? Those who took part in the battles of Sedan, Dinant, and elsewhere testify that they saw next to nothing of the French Air Force and that they were abandoned to the Stuka attacks and that this contributed more than anything else to the demoralization of our troops. And yet our fighters gave a good account of themselves. Their successes prove that. But they fought dispersed over a wide front. General D'Astier de la Vigerie noted in despair on May 15: "My fighters are everywhere, sent without heed to our dislocated armies!" As for Allied bombers, we saw their spirit of self-sacrifice at Sedan on May 14.

"How, then, could the participants in the drama assert in good faith that they saw no French planes?" wrote de la Vigerie. "I believe this can be explained by the complete state of numbness caused by the Stuka attacks and by the difficulty of identifying French planes at medium altitudes." One must also add that our troops in general saw nothing of the air battles because they mostly took place well forward of or behind the front line. They were concerned only with the Stukas which fell upon their positions, where the real battle was being fought.

Errors in organization and employment. Why was the sky clear for the Stukas? The first reason was the disparity in strength, but this was not such as to prevent our air force from having some influence on the battle. "On the whole, our fighters were good," wrote Gamelin, "and we had faith in them." Then there were our losses through *Flak*, enemy raids, and, finally, there was the meagerness of the British contribution.

Was not our ineffectiveness in the battle due to the same mistakes in organization and employment as were made with the armor?

The whole German air might was concentrated into two air fleets and a general reserve. In all probability each of the two air fleets operated in the zone of one of the army groups (A and B), but without being under the command of the army group. This meant that they could not be whittled away by having to answer every call from the army. As for the general reserve, which comprised all the Stukas and all the airborne troops, this remained securely in the hands of the German High Command, a weapon for the mortal blow, at the right time and the right place.

We, on the contrary, allotted a large portion of our aircraft a priori to army formations. Colonel de Lesquen wrote: "Our two mistakes were the breaking down of the organic whole of our fighter strength through army demands, and the creation [in army formations] of Air Observation Groups (G.A.O.) of inordinate size."

What is more, the very composition of our Air Command Headquarters turned it into a veritable bottleneck. The Northeast Front was divided into Zones of Air Operations (Z.O.A.) following the boundaries of the army groups, and under the orders of the officer commanding the Air Cooperation Forces (General Têtu), who was near General Georges. The two sets of orders would sometimes be contradictory. Furthermore, the officer commanding the Reserve Air Force had some formations operating in Z.O.A. without being under the orders of the Zone Commander. The officers commanding fighter groups allocated to the army were themselves tugged two ways by the army air force commanders and the fighter group commanders, whose respective spheres of authority were badly defined. The result of this was contradictory orders—or no orders at all!

In addition, our Air Command, thinking it had plenty of time, did not cast its fighter reserves into the Meuse sector during the decisive battle on May 13 "for fear of engaging them too soon." Finally, our fighters were engaged in escorting bombers and air observation planes. Thus in spite of its quality, the air force was frittered away and became ineffective.

The Luftwaffe, on the contrary, was always on the offensive, and concentrated, following the principle of *Schwerpunkt,* which Kesselring interpreted in the following words: "The possibility of victory lay in concentrating our whole air might on a single objective."

Two examples are particularly striking. On May 13 the Germans put 700 planes in the air over Sedan, 200 of which were Stukas; we shall see how successful they were. But on the next day the *Schwerpunkt* was elsewhere, and there was not a single German plane in that sector, the air defense of which was left to *Flak.*

On our side, on the tragic morning of May 15, the general commanding the Z.O.A. allocated to the First Army Group received from the Group Commander the order to dispose his fighters as follows: 60 percent for Touchon's detachment, 30 percent to the Second Army, 5 percent to the Ninth Army, and 5 percent to the Seventh Army. Within the hour he received from General Têtu different disposal instructions for the same fighters: 50 percent for the Mézières area, 30 percent for the Sedan area, and 20 percent for the Dinant area. During this time direct and pressing appeals were coming in from the various armies.

Other Deficiencies

Anti-aircraft defense. Another handicap for our airmen was the fact that they came across thick and very active *Flak* resistance, whereas the German pilots were able to operate more or less unmolested owing to a lack of effective anti-aircraft defenses on our side. On May 10, *Flak* could number 9,300 guns; 6,700 of 37 mm and 2,600 of 88 mm. Our anti-aircraft defense had only 1,200 guns of 20 or 25 mm and 370 of 75 mm inherited from 1918.

Dive-bombers. Even though the Stukas had already shown their worth in Spain, notably at Guadalajara in 1937, and even though

Vuillemin at General Milch's invitation in 1938 had watched an impressive display of dive-bombing, our High Command both air and army did not see fit to adopt this type of warfare. Our prototype, the Loire-Nieuport, comparable with the Stuka had been manufactured in 1938 and an order for 120 of them had been given, 70 for the navy and 50 for the air force, but the air force cancelled the order "for technical not tactical reasons," as Colonel de Lesquen put it, as the machine seemed "slow, vulnerable, and not steady enough." But the Stukas themselves had these defects, and this did not prevent them from playing a very important part at the beginning of the war, as much by the damage they inflicted on material in depots, lines of communication, and gun batteries as by their shattering effect on the morale of unseasoned troops.

Our leaders believed they could improve on the dive-bombers by the use of the medium "assault bomber" operating at almost ground-level. One brigade was formed and equipped with the Bréguet 691. "But," wrote General Seive, "the first operational flight they made in Belgium on May 12 sounded the knell of these 'hedgehoppers,' as they are too vulnerable to small-arms fire, especially if they have not surprise on their side."

Airborne troops. As for airborne operations: "Neither the Army nor the Air Staff," wrote Colonel Rogé, "had really understood their importance, which explained our complete lack of air-transport facilities."

Conclusion. In the same way as our armor had been conceived only as auxiliary to infantry, our air force had been regarded not as a weapon with which to combat the Luftwaffe but as auxiliary to the army, to afford it air protection. Hence the dispersion of effort in these two new arms, and consequently their ineffectiveness in a brief war which the enemy intended to win by launching all his land and air forces in one concentrated onslaught against our army.

However, this type of concentration caused great wear and tear to its strategic air force during cooperation with the army, and although it won for Germany the first battle, she might well have lost the war! What would have become of the Luftwaffe if the Battle of France had lasted a long time? To give us some idea of this, we must first of all glance at the initial state of the enemy air force, and then the condition of the two air forces after the first battle.

"Granted," wrote General von Lossberg, "on the surface the German Air Force appeared unrivalled, but one was not supposed to go deeper! As a war-machine, the Luftwaffe was even less prepared than the army. In 1939 it was all it could do to form up the front-line units for reserves, and even stocks of spare parts were completely lacking. So long as the Luftwaffe was only called upon to carry out limited operations, replacements from industry could just about keep pace with losses, but the gravity of the situation was painfully obvious later." General Tippelskirch, in fact, pointed out the disproportion between line and reserve formations.

We, in 1940, had no idea of the wastage rate in the German Air Force. Kesselring put it in these words: "From May 13 continuous operations had literally consumed all the personnel and material of our air force. After three weeks, units fell to 50 percent and even 30 percent of establishment."

After Dunkirk the 2nd Air Fleet had lost 450 aircraft. By the end of August, after the Battle of France and before that of Britain, "the Luftwaffe was in bad shape," wrote Colonel Baumbach, "for its crews had been lost"; and Kesselring tells us that there were no more than 700 planes among the fighter squadrons. A tribute to the achievements of Allied pilots.

Naturally, Goering declared that he had had no need to use the 1,000 planes of the 1st and 4th Air Fleets, and he showed neutral correspondents aircraft allegedly belonging to these unimpaired air groups. But coming from this "master bluffer," the demonstration proves nothing at all.

On our side, as the unexpected result of not having used our reserves, our 1,450 planes of the interior formed a reinforcement which was still available in June. At the same time our industrial output was rising sharply. So much so that General Vuillemin in his book says: "At the time of the Armistice, the French Air Force was ready to carry on, as it had a greater front-line effective strength than on May 10."

One may well imagine, then, that if we had held the enemy at the Meuse, and if the Battle of France had gone on longer, superiority in the air would have been ours! The Luftwaffe had grown too quickly for enduring strength. As General Rieckhoff says: "Quickly made, quickly unmade. Sooner or later every bluff is called!" And he adds:

"From 1939 until 1944 no foreign estimate had correctly assessed the strength of the Luftwaffe. No one suspected how low it really was."

In point of fact, after achieving its morale effects of surprise and terror at Sedan and Dinant on unseasoned and insufficiently trained troops, the Luftwaffe was powerless to interfere seriously with our strategic moves; as, for instance, the Dunkirk evacuation. It no longer made a great impression on our troops at the Aisne, and its weaknesses were exposed to the full light of day in the Battle of Britain.

Artillery

Superiority of French guns. On the eve of the battle our army had some 11,200 guns of calibers between 75 and 280 mm, of which 5,600 were 75s; 1,600, 105s; 2,000 short 155s; 1,200 long 155s; and 680 heavy guns of 220 and 280 mm. An improvement on the old design had been effected by the adoption of the new Brandt shells which increased the range of our 75s from 7 to 8 miles and also increased the range of our 105s and 155s by one and a quarter miles.

Such was our artillery, "the principal arm of the French," according to the German generals, who had a great respect for it. "The French had a great deal of heavy and very heavy artillery," wrote General von Tippelskirch, "and, although some of it was obsolescent, it could have put down a crushing weight of fire."

In May, German field artillery (at the front and in the interior) consisted of 7,710 guns, of which 5,380 were 105 mm and 2,330, 150 mm. Their heavy artillery consisted of 124 mortars of 220 mm.

Inferiority of organization. Unfortunately, our artillery was only formidable in the static warfare that we had prepared for, and it was a complete failure in the mobile war imposed on us by the Germans. Its main drawback lay in its method of propulsion, which was mainly horsedrawn. This made our units very susceptible to air attack while on the move, and prevented almost all movement during the course of a battle, which resulted in wholesale abandonment of material as soon as the retreat started.

But it was chiefly an error of doctrine which handicapped our artillery. It was inflexible and designed for static warfare. In his remarkable work, General Menu wrote:

The conduct of gunner officers and men is not in question. Only those who made our artillery conform to outmoded patterns of warfare are to blame. It made its reappearance in 1930–1940 with the same materials, the same organization, and the same methods as in 1918. We opposed an enemy who relied on speed with a weapon designed to reduce fortified positions, a weapon which had sacrificed rapidity of fire for the sake of accuracy, and had become dominated by mathematical calculations. These heavy guns were ideal for slow, methodical and lengthy bombardments, capable of battering down concrete works, barbed wire, gun emplacements and all other static targets; but how would they fare against elusive armored vehicles, moving with extreme agility?

With its existing apparatus and ammunition stocks, our artillery needed a considerable period of time to take up its positions and even to get out of them. That is why we saw our guns abandoned on the battlefield or lining the sides of the roads, often without having fired a shot. "We expected," wrote General Menu, "that the powerful artillery organization set up above the divisions would play a dominating decisive part in the battle. It collapsed without being used!"

The 75 mm was the only gun which was still of any great use, but mostly in the anti-tank role, which was not the purpose for which it had been designed.

As for the enemy, they almost completely dispensed with artillery in their thrusts on the Meuse, using dive-bombers, and the direct, observed fire of tank, anti-tank, and anti-aircraft guns. But this does not mean that it was impossible for our artillery to play a decisive role in this battle. Indeed, it would have done so had we only been able and willing to use it as the Russians did a little while later.

The Navy

In Germany. The Treaty of Versailles had allowed Germany to keep 6 old ships of the line, 6 light cruisers, and 74 smaller craft. New ships as replacements were restricted to maximum tonnage of 10,000 for ships of the line (which resulted in the famous "pocket battleships") and 6,000 for cruisers. However, a naval treaty concluded with Britain in 1935 authorized Germany to raise her total tonnage to 35 percent of that of the British fleet.

But it was not until September 1938 when Hitler, together with Admiral Raeder, envisaged the possibility of conflict with Britain, that Hitler set up a commission with the task of working out the first real naval rearmament program. Thus it was that the "Z Plan," wholly offensive in nature, did not emerge until the beginning of 1939. This program conceived the creation of two task forces, each consisting of 3 ships of the line, 1 aircraft carrier, and many cruisers, destroyers, and submarines, which were designed to sever Britain's lifelines on the ocean.

By the time war was declared this program had scarcely been set in motion and many ships existed only on paper. "On mobilization," wrote General von Tippelskirch, "we ought not to have dreamt of sticking to our schedule for the construction of large ships not due to be completed before 1944. The navy should have confined itself to completing ships which were nearly ready, and concentrated its efforts on submarine construction. Unlike conditions in 1914, Germany in 1939 was ill-prepared for a war against Britain."

On September 1, 1939, the German fleet consisted of 2 battle-cruisers of 26,000 tons (*Scharnhorst* and *Gneisenau*); 3 pocket battle-ships (*Deutschland, Admiral Scheer,* and *Admiral Graf Spee*); 2 heavy cruisers (*Hipper* and *Blucher*); 6 light cruisers, 22 destroyers, 27 long-range submarines of 500 to 700 tons, and 30 coastal submarines of 250 tons. Not a single aircraft-carrier as yet existed. Two ships of the line (*Bismarck* and *Tirpitz*) and 1 heavy cruiser (*Prince Eugen*) were still being built in the shipyards.

In order to see the significance of these figures, one must compare them with the Allied totals. Against 13 large warships, the Allies had 107: 17 battleships, of which 7 were French; 7 aircraft-carriers (1 French); 83 cruisers (19 French). The Germans had 27 long-range submarines, but the Allies had 175 (78 French). The comparison is eloquent, and one understands how Admiral Friedrich Ruge could write: "The German Navy was facing a disastrous situation and it absolutely lacked the means to deal with it."

One curious point was that the "Z Plan" was mainly concerned with the larger ships which had no chance of being completed in 1939, 1940, or even in 1941, and which would have to be abandoned in a war against Britain when the greatest need was for submarines. "Had Hitler been considering a war against Britain," concludes General von Lossberg, "he would have orientated his naval construction industry and would have given greatest priority to submarines."

In France. The spirit of a service reflects that of its leader. The head of the French Navy, both in authority and prestige, stood head and shoulders above the army and air force chiefs. He molded the French Navy, which he considered as his very own, into a magnificent body, in cohesion and training. Whatever criticisms one may have against the subsequent actions of the Admiral of the Fleet, they in no way diminish his merit in fashioning such a good weapon for his country.

In its materiel our navy was first-rate. Its two ships of the line, the *Dunkerque* and the *Strasbourg,* could match the pocket battleships in speed and armament. Its 32 light cruisers were among the fastest in the world. It had the most powerful submarine fleet, and 2 battleships of 35,000 tons, the *Richelieu* and the *Jean-Bart,* were nearing completion. "For generations," declared Mr. Churchill in the House of Commons in November 1939, "the French Navy has not been so powerful or so efficient."

This shows that, given determination, it was quite possible to build up a strong war-machine between the wars, whether at sea, on the land, or in the air. Unfortunately, in the struggle against Germany, the best service had a very secondary role, but which it nevertheless accomplished brilliantly in cordial collaboration with the Royal Navy.

Conclusion

Such were our weapons compared with those of the Germans. Palpably equal to theirs in September 1939, they could have enabled us at least to hold them successfully in the spring of 1940 had a serious effort been made to improve them during the "phony war," and most of all if they had been properly used. As M. Henri Michel puts it: "The inequality was not in the armed forces facing each other as much as the manner in which they were employed." This faulty employment was a direct result of our outmoded war doctrines inherited from the 1914–1918 war, and our tendency to conservatism after our victory.

This is how a great and victorious army, which had had every opportunity to maintain and modernize its strength, came to be beaten by an army which had been defeated, suppressed for seventeen years, and then hastily reconstructed!

This is how an *élite* of 150,000 young men, detaching itself from this improvised army and led by an Austrian reservist corporal, could, in a few days, destroy a traditional army of 5 million men led by its Great War leaders under the aegis of a glorious Field-Marshal.

This is how Defeat was born of Victory.

General André Beaufre
THE DOWNFALL SEEN FROM GHQ

Born in 1902, André Beaufre began his military career in 1923 when he graduated from Saint-Cyr. Over and beyond professional services and achievements, which were to earn him his country's highest decorations and the rank of Full General by the time he retired in 1961, his many books and articles have won him additional laurels as one of the keenest French military minds of the post-World War I period. His position as a staff officer attached to General Headquarters in May-June, 1940, gave him a unique vantage point from which to observe the disintegration of the French Army. The sharp contrast between General Beaufre's verdict and the thesis advanced by Colonel Goutard bears witness to the complexity of the question.

On the morning of 10 May I was woken by the sound of bombs, as was most of the French Army. Now we were emerging from the long period of torpor and daydreams which I have to tried to describe. Now the war of waiting was over; now the battle was about to begin after twenty years of preparation. Destiny on that lovely May morning had come to confront us with the pitiless proof of hard facts. I think that few of the actors in this immense tragedy were unaware of how vital was this moment, so full of imponderables.

Even today when I try to describe the extraordinary events which followed, a flood of mixed images and feelings pours through my mind. Nightmare is a word not strong enough to describe the memory which remains so bitterly clear. This few weeks' campaign,

From General André Beaufre, *1940: The Fall of France,* tr. Desmond Flower (New York, 1968), pp. 179–180; 197–200; 202–209; 212–215. Copyright © 1967 by Cassell and Company Ltd. Reprinted by permission of Cassell and Company Ltd., and Alfred A. Knopf, Inc.

which led to a defeat so total and so sudden, was from first to last an endless surprise exposing our inability to cope with the enemy's torrential advance or find any answer to it. Like a bad dream, the enemy's forces were everywhere, striking at will with diabolical freedom, while our feet remained rooted to the ground and we seemed constrained by a thousand invisible bonds which slowed down all our movements. But scarcely had such movements got under way than they were rendered useless by the collapse of the dispositions which it was hoped would limit the disaster. With a desperate effort a fresh deployment would be organized, but once more the machine could not answer to what was required of it, nothing could be done in the time available and the defeat grew and grew at an alarming pace. The men who were witnessing and living through this drama beneath a cloudless sky did so with stupor and dejection, but could not bring themselves to believe that this was real, that France was dying and that something would not happen to save us at the last moment. But nothing did come and destiny inexorably crushed us more and more every moment. The helpless ship was making water through every seam, could no longer answer the helm, and the terrifying waves were battering her old worm-eaten hull.

I want to describe this terrible atmosphere in which I was not living with the fighting troops, but in an absurd succession of châteaux, in order to explain the reasons. Details of the battles come better from the historians than from me because they have more complete documentation; impressions of the fighting and of the defeat belong to eyewitnesses. My object is only to show why we were beaten and how the military instrument of which we have seen the build-up was commanded in the searching test of battle. This terrible lesson will not have been useless if we can draw from it a lesson for the future. . . .

History's judgment must be passed upon those few days: the French Army was nothing more than a vast inefficient tool, incapable of quick reaction or adaptation, quite incapable of taking the offensive or of any mobility. We were reaping the logical consequences of twenty years of ill-conceived doctrine aggravated by the nine months of somnolence which made up for us the first period of the war. In other words in May 1940 we showed ourselves to be just as cumbersome and just as immature as we were during the first skirmishes in Lorraine in 1939. Much discussion has gone on over the reason for our defeat. There has been much talk of shortcomings in equipment, morale and command. Certainly all these factors played their part and helped in our downfall, but the end was inevitable because, faced by an able and swift-moving adversary, our Army could not find any answer even when it enjoyed numerical superiority. The machine was old and rusty. A repetition of the Marne was impossible, however great the qualities of the commander.

This knowledge bore down bitterly upon our minds from the first days of June in 1940.

In these nightmare days, interest was centered on Dunkirk. The news was terrible; there was indescribable chaos on the beaches. The British were evacuating their troops in priority under constant bombardment from the air. For some inexplicable reason the German armored divisions did not attack (we knew after the war that it was the decision of Hitler to spare Great Britain in the hope of a compromise peace), but the situation was more and more critical. Like everyone else we followed the drama by telephone. At the end I spoke for the last time via England with Admiral Abrial, commanding the fortress at Dunkirk. Weygand came into my office and seized the telephone, could not hear well, and seized the second receiver, kneeling among lines on the floor; "Abrial, you've got to hold on . . . hold on." We were cut off. He remained prostrate for a moment, then got up sharply; I admired this old man who carried on his frail shoulders the crushing weight of a lost campaign.

At the end of May the situation was grave but we had succeeded in re-forming a front from the Channel to Switzerland. The northern half of our forces, more than sixty Allied divisions, was surrounded and thrown into the sea. The 300,000 men who were saved (only 100,000 of them French) were nothing more than a mob without arms who took no further part in the battle. We were left with no more than sixty divisions and barely a few hundred tanks scattered along a hastily constructed front from the Channel to the Swiss border. Only in the east we leaned upon the Maginot Line which was intact. What was our strategy now to be?

The choice was a difficult one. One wonders, and one will go on wondering more and more, if it would not have been better to stage a fighting withdrawal, playing for time and watching for a fresh chance to stand. This theory seems attractive and will find more supporters as the realities of the actual moment sink into the past. But there were several determining reasons which militated against this heroic solution. The main one, in my opinion, was the inability to maneuver which our troops had just displayed on the Somme. With so inefficient a weapon, was it wise voluntarily to give ground in the hope that the enemy would eventually make a mistake, of which we would not be able to take advantage anyway? Furthermore any withdrawal would undoubtedly cost us Paris and the Maginot Line, two moral factors of prime importance. No one at the time could visualize such sacrifice without one more fight.

Our commanders, haunted by memories of March 1918, thought that they could survive the German penetration once again. What they felt should be done was to tighten up their forces and cover Paris. One might say: "Haven't they yet learnt that static defense is valueless against tanks?" Yes and no. We had watched with stupefaction the collapse of our Armies on the Meuse, but this failure was attributed to the moral surprise and bad anti-tank defense. But there was still an idea that now, after the first baptism of fire, the defense against armor would recover the efficiency it had shown in peacetime exercises. It was not a question of revolution but of simple adaptation. One immediate reaction was to try to reorganize the defense into strong-points made up of infantry and artillery. It was what was called then the "quadrillage,"* a discontinuous tactical disposition of a greater depth than the one used previously, and by which General Weygand felt that he might check the Panzer divisions, if everyone followed the formula and really fought "like beasts." For twenty years we had relied upon the value of defense; it was impossible to change our outlook overnight.

In any case—and here I am on delicate ground—I do not believe that by this time our high command had any further hope of success; the constant series of rebuffs which they had suffered, the constant surprises, the disappointments which followed every attempt to rally, had broken the spirit of our leaders; if defeat was not already accepted as inevitable, it was certainly regarded as just around the

---

* This method of defense was used by the British in the Western Desert and there referred to as the "box" system (trs.).

corner. This mental outlook which had become obvious in some quarters from 14 May had spread despite the dynamic action of General Weygand. Weygand himself, a doctor called in at the last moment to heal a man dying of an incurable disease, had done his best; but fundamentally he must have felt that he had little chance of success. On 29 May in fact he made it known to the Government that "a moment may well come when France, however willing, may find it impossible to continue military operations in defense of her homeland." This mental reservation which he was expressing was common throughout Headquarters and this fate was generally considered to be inescapable. But before that everything had to be done to check the enemy. We felt ourselves beaten but no one would admit it until our defeat was absolute. It seemed that thus the honor of our arms would be saved.

I have tried to give some idea of the atmosphere in which the next phase of the battle was prepared during the breathing-space which the agony of Dunkirk allowed us. It is difficult to describe such complex and dramatic feelings, when no one uttered more than a part of what was in his mind and documents were prepared with systematic optimism. Furthermore the reactions of individuals were widely different. The general view was that defeat was probable but that we must try everything, and perhaps another defensive battle would bring success. In this supreme trial, we held to the only maneuver of which our Army was capable, to which all our reflexes were conditioned: to stand our ground "without any question of withdrawal from the positions which we now occupy," as General Weygand ordered with his usual clarity and energy on 26 May.

. . . In spite of this the position was not completely restored. The compromise which emerged was to put into the line divisions which until now had been held in reserve, but to replace them in the rear with troops who were coming in later. By 5 June between the sea and the Oise there were eleven divisions in contact, but in the rear there were six infantry divisions and six more of armor or cavalry, the latter very experienced but short of material. This staggering of resources, absolutely contrary to General Weygand's intentions, might be considered justified with counter-attack in mind, but in fact, as time was to show, it was a mental preparation for further retreat. Thus once more Weygand was unable to get his orders carried out.

Meanwhile great hopes were placed in the change in our defensive tactics: the adoption of the "all-round defense" (the "quadrillage") based on woods or villages, strengthened with field-pieces in an anti-tank role, tactics which Doumenc had recommended and Weygand had adopted with enthusiasm. This was the state of affairs on 5 June when, according to Hitler's grandiloquent announcement "the greatest offensive of modern times" was launched. I got the news very early on the telephone and immediately told Weygand and Doumenc. The information coming in was encouraging. Our troops, whose morale had risen and who believed that there were substantial reserves behind them, fought magnificently. Almost everywhere the strong-points held, even when surrounded, and the German attack lost its impetus.

These almost unexpected results brought a gleam of hope. Would the "quadrillage" tactics and the determination which had come back to us succeed in breaking the terrible spell which for more than a month had been cast over our Army? Nevertheless our positions were in danger in several places. We needed to throw in our reserves to counter-attack. It had always been Weygand's idea that our greatest effort should be concentrated on the Somme. It was this which was uppermost in his mind when on the night of 5/6 June he realized that the directions given by Third Army Group were in "direct contradiction" of his formal orders. Early on the morning of the 6th Weygand ordered me to summon to a council of war in his office General Georges, General Doumenc and General Besson —commanding Third Army Group—and I wondered if Besson was not on the verge of being relieved of his command.

When they came out from Weygand's office I hurried up to Doumenc and asked him what decisions had been taken; to my great surprise he replied, "Besson spoke up for himself very well."

"What," I said, "it's to be delaying action maneuver?" Doumenc nodded.

I was staggered. How could this be? For ten days General Weygand had been laying down and holding to a plan in which he believed. This plan so far had stood up with remarkable success because nowhere had our positions been driven in, yet here he was giving up all he believed without any contrary proof! It was a catastrophe because the strong-points, if they withdrew, would have to abandon their major equipment and would completely lose confidence in their ability to hold on. This was opening the way to a rout which could only grow faster and faster.

Once more this brings home sharply how difficult it is for a commander to impose his way of thinking. Once he has made his decision known, everything conspires against him; on top of the doubts which must exist in his own mind are piled the information coming in of the course of the operation and the objections of his subordinates. Napoleon said "It is difficult to realize the strength of will which is needed to fight a battle." Weygand's strength of will was undeniable yet twice, on 24 May and 6 June, he found himself forced to abandon his first intentions.

This new concept did not become apparent on the 6th except in one phrase in the order he issued congratulating the troops on their magnificent resistance: "After the movements now being carried out *which will replace* our forces now locked in action with the enemy. . . ." But in effect it led to our keeping our reserves where they were and ruled out any counter-attack in strength, and from the 7th orders were given within the Armies to pull back, entailing the abandonment of all heavy equipment within the strong-points. The battle "with no thought of withdrawal" had lasted forty-eight hours.

My remaining memories of this ill-fated period are no more than incidents, flashes each more depressing than the last.

On the 7th I went with Doumenc to the Command Post of the Seventh Army near Forges-les-Eaux. On the way, through a countryside already devoid of its inhabitants, we watched with a kind of fascinated horror a German fighter literally murder one of our cumbersome fighter-bombers, which fluttered slowly down in flames. When we reached the command post other enemy aircraft were flying over it and the officers were out in the streets shooting at them with small arms in a sort of frustrated rage. The Germans had broken through in the Rouen-Soissons area. On the 8th the order was given by Third Army Group to withdraw to the Seine and the so-called Paris line.

At General Georges's command post, at Bondons, the atmosphere had become unbearable. At the switchboard, which was receiving bad news at monotonous one-minute intervals, there was no longer any reaction: one officer would acknowledge messages in a quiet, soft voice, another with an almost hysterical giggle—"Ah, yes, your left has been driven in; oh, I see, they're in behind you. I'll make a note of it!" Everyone else in the room, prostrate and silent, was sitting about in armchairs.

In the morning when I was marking up the wall map I was watched by the Major-General Ops., a firm and proud instructor when I had been at Saint-Cyr; he wept openly, his face screwed up like a baby's. In this horrible atmosphere I tried to keep a hold on myself, forcing myself to keep calm and do my job as efficiently as I could.

Alas, on the 9th the enemy offensive spread eastwards into the Rethel area against the front of Fourth Army Group, brought together to hold the gap formed by the flat country of Champagne, and made rapid progress. By the following day the front was completely broken; the Germans exploited their success with deep thrusts and had already reached the Seine between Rouen and the Oise, fanning out south of Soissons and isolating our right wing by a drive from Rethel towards the Seine. Our entire defensive disposition west of the Maginot Line was dislocated and we had no more reserves. This time all hope was gone, the game was up, and nothing could save us.

We would have to leave Montry, as the Government was leaving Paris. The first move visualized was a short one, to the Loire: we would go to Briare and the Government to Tours (shades of 1871). Our monstrous GHQ could hardly be described as mobile. It was not a movement in the military sense but a household removal.

Weygand took us with him to Paris where he was to have a last meeting with the Government. He sent them a note: "The events of the last two days' fighting make it incumbent on me to inform M. le Président du Conseil that the collapse of our lines of defense must be expected at any moment" [it had already occurred]. "If this should come about, our troops will continue to fight until their means and their strength are exhausted, but their complete dissolution can only be a matter of time." This grave communication was unfortunately an understatement and did not bring out the full tragedy of the situation. The reservations in the mind of the Commander-in-Chief are understandable, but they nevertheless contributed to keeping alive baseless illusions in the minds of the Government.

During this time, off the record we were bringing ourselves to talk about bringing the debacle to an end before the whole country was overrun. The word "armistice" was first used, if I remember right, at Vincennes, in Gamelin's erstwhile command post. We had just learned that Italy proposed to enter the war. While we were having lunch in the officers' mess the crackling radio picked up an Italian broadcast—a speech, cheers from the crowd and *giovinezza*. This gesture of "political realism" was the last straw. Were we to go on and on to total disaster? There was at that time—and I write as a witness—no thought of suing Germany for peace, but only of stopping the fighting, the literal meaning of the word "armistice."

Subsequently there has been a great deal of despondent talk about the birth of this armistice which I have never understood. I do not want to get involved here in this argument, conclusions on which will belong to history when all the facts are available. I will confine myself, as I have tried to do up till now, to describing the atmosphere in which we found ourselves and the state of mind which resulted. The idea of some long prepared "treason" springs from a sordid imagination and has no basis in fact, as these pages have shown. The argument which was to develop in the next few days between Weygand and Reynaud on the relative merits of an armistice and of capitulation, seems to me equally pointless. Whatever way one looks at it, we had tried and we had lost. Without admitting complete defeat, it was essential to disengage and wait for better times. To argue the toss in the midst of defeat made no sense; the only thing which mattered was to find a way of disengaging.

Weygand came back from his meeting with the Government in a highly nervous state. Paris was already very empty. Everywhere archives were being burnt and a pall of thick black smoke from the oil storage tanks of Havre, which were being destroyed, put the first gray sky over the city in a spring which had been endlessly beautiful.

The march table allowed for our leaving Paris in a special train which was drawn up in Vincennes station. The idea of a special train was a good one because the roads were hopelessly congested, but I feared that we might be strafed from the air. But nothing happened and we carried our misery away in sumptuous drawing-room cars.

At Briare the command post was set up in the Château du Muguet, a stuffy house at the bottom of a damp valley. Communications were unreliable, but good enough for us to follow the progress of the Germans' inexorable advance. Often the best way of finding out if a town had been taken was to ring up the Post Office where the switchboard operators, who devotedly stuck to their posts, would say if the Germans had arrived or not.

The Château du Muguet is associated in my mind with two important memories: the first concerns General de Gaulle who for several days had been Under Secretary of State for War. One of my main tasks was to keep him informed of the progress of operations. Unfortunately the news which I had to telephone to him was absolutely horrifying and the General, who, like all of us, was suffering bitterly, listened to my recitals as if I were personally responsible. I remember one day when I reported that our Armies had been cut to ribbons by the German penetration, he said to me severely, "You have no right to say that." Perhaps not, but. . . .

It was about this time that there was born the idea of the "Breton Redoubt," of which General de Gaulle has in his Memoirs denied paternity—yet one cannot help thinking that it must have had some connection with his desire to ignore defeat and to do something "come what might." Naturally the Breton Redoubt was stillborn. Soon after we were asked to work out a plan for transporting all the recruits under instruction to North Africa. We had neither the ships nor the organization to carry out an operation (involving 300,000 men) so important, so difficult and of doubtful value. In fact in the general mental disarray the majority sank into fatalism or despair and those who retained any feeling of hope were few and far between. In the midst of a thousand difficulties de Gaulle was to build his reputation on a proud refusal to recognize the sad realities of the present, but this refusal made no sense until it could be based upon and allied to the British determination to continue the fight. In France in 1940 the will for war, which had never been particularly strong, was completely shattered.

My second memory is of the last meeting of the Supreme Franco-

British Council which was held at the Château du Muguet. All the heads of the coalition were there: on the British side Churchill, Eden, Alan Brooke and Spears; on the French side Reynaud, Pétain, Weygand, Darlan, Vuillemin and Doumenc, Baudouin and de Gaulle. The conference was to take place after dinner and the General's ADC had spent a long time on the table plan.

Before dinner, in the drawing-room, Paul Reynaud, utterly exhausted and a bundle of nerves, walked up and down, twitching in a way which I have never seen since. Pétain was Olympian. Darlan solid and cunning. Eden seemed to me rather fragile and a little *"fin de race."* Churchill, dynamic as always, held court solidly settled in an armchair. I remember a moment when Spears went across to him and said that he would like to introduce de Gaulle to him and then went off to bring the General across—"General de Gaulle whom I have mentioned to you." In his Memoirs the General speaks of a previous interview with Churchill. They had already met. But I must bear witness to the fact that the first real contact between them was on this evening. Their conversation was very lively and when we rose to go in to dinner Churchill said in his own particular brand of French: "I have had a very interesting conversation with General de Gaulle and I would like to keep him next to me." The table plan, worked out with so much care, was in ruins . . . but on these ruins were built the first foundations of the Liberation.

After the meal was over the conference took place in the dining-room. The subjects for discussion were numerous. Our immediate problem was to get more help from the United Kingdom, particularly in the air. Churchill offered *one* division, and made some play out of future help from America. He did what he could, but very loyally he made it plain that he was not prepared to disperse the RAF which was and had to be an essential instrument in the defense of the British Isles.

The description which Weygand gave him of the general picture underlined the gravity of the whole situation. On the front facing the Alps our troops were victoriously resisting without difficulty, but on the German frontier the situation was rapidly deteriorating. Our forces to the north and north-west of Paris, apart from those concentrated round Havre, were pulling out as best they could, abandoning most of their material as they went. Their collapse, which had already begun, could only accelerate. But their line of retreat was still open. On the other hand the German offensive which had broken through in Champagne was turning towards the Jura and was about to devolve upon our Army Group East, still holding the Maginot Line; this would represent the same threat of encirclement which we had already experienced around Abbeville. Time was pressing if we were not to lose our last intact Army Group.

The battle in the north had cost us thirty-five divisions, the battle of the Somme had either destroyed or broken up twenty to twenty-five more divisions. We now had left to us no more than some forty divisions for the whole western front. There was only one answer which had been decided upon that morning and accepted by the Government: this was a general withdrawal, and the first step was back to a line drawn from Caen, the Loire, the Côte d'Or, to the Jura.

Churchill tried to combat these disastrous indications by recalling the precedent of 25 March 1918, but Pétain interpolated that in 1918 he had needed forty divisions simply to close the gap: that is to say as much as the maximum remaining forces now available of the French Army. We were lost because we had no further reserves. Then Churchill, very serious, said that he understood that France might well have to give up the fight, but, if that should come about, he wished to make it plain that Great Britain would relentlessly pursue the struggle to its very end.

The conference ended without any further definite decisions: it was agreed that France would hold on for a few more days as she slipped down to the depths. The British, thanks to their island fastness, would not give up. But was there any reason why the Germans should not be able to effect a landing? Churchill neither accepted nor formally objected to the idea of French capitulation, which from our side had still not been put to him as an unavoidable eventuality. The real detailed discussion between the military command and the Government was to begin the next day at Cangé, near Tours.

Churchill went to bed—late. A bottle of brandy had been put on his bedside table and it was found to be empty in the morning, after he had appeared in a red dressing-gown at the top of the staircase shouting for his valet because the bath-water was not hot enough.

On our side, our worries over the fate of our Army Group East after the breakthrough in Champagne, together with the disintegration of our front from the Channel to the Marne, forced two decisions upon us on the 12th: a general order to withdraw, and the abandonment of the Maginot Line. Almost simultaneously Paris was declared an open city in order to avoid its destruction. General Dentz was sent in to acknowledge the Germans on their arrival.

For all of us the battle was over. From that day on General Headquarters abandoned its Olympian role and came down to the level of every Frenchman: in other words they were just refugees on the road. . . .

The collapse of the French Army is the most important event of the twentieth century. Our downfall upset the balance which had been built up and maintained through the ages. Europe, the mother of modern civilization, found itself deprived of its western counterbalance. The destruction of Germany which was to come left in place of the traditional Europe only a zone of weakness, while the USA and the USSR, now overwhelming powers, disputed between themselves the dominance of the world which Europe had lost, and which led inevitably to the fashion for decolonization.

All this grew out of the thinking of our military leaders and the courage of our soldiers. If they had been more effective the face of the world today would be different.

Thus, before the bar of history, we have a terrible responsibility.

I have tried to describe, in all its complexity, the chain of causes which led to our downfall. Contrary to various biased theses which have been put forward, it is apparent that everyone was in some degree party to what happened. That is the way it goes in great historical events.

On the stage of the world all the major actors contributed to the drama: Great Britain by her prolonged blindness to what was happening in Germany, the United States by their selfish isolation after 1918, Italy by her illusions of grandeur, the Soviet by her Fabian duplicity, even Japan with her ambitions of modernized barbarism.

In France the first fatal germs go back to 1914–1918 which by its useless slaughter produced the pacifism of the *"ancien combattant,"* the duality of the Foch-Pétain thinking after the war, and above all the narrow conquerors' dogmatism of the Pétain school of thought. From then on, diplomatic wavering, the muddle of internal politics, the general atrophy of the state and all its ingredients could only make matters worse. Neither the French "fascists" nor the *Front Populaire* was responsible for our downfall, although they may have contributed to it.

By 1940 there was nothing to be done: fate had stacked the cards too heavily against us. Even had we had a Napoleon to lead us, we might not have avoided defeat but the disaster would have been kept within bounds. This was because there was no one who could make the huge military machine which we had at our disposal move itself, as I have tried to show by describing the events which took place on the Somme between 25 May and 6 June.

How could we have avoided defeat? It is possible that the last chance was thrown away when we refused to make war in 1939. If we had really assaulted the Siegfried Line we would have trained our troops, rejuvenated the high command, tried out our methods of combat and put new life into the war effort. The battle of 1940 would have been fought with a few more cards in our hand. If in addition we had had the great military leader whom we lacked, we might not have won, but we would not have lost. But certain shortfalls—particularly in armament and aviation—were already inevitable and liable to prove deadly dangerous.

This is why the climactic moment of the drama was really long before, before the Russian incident, before Munich. Actually it was in March 1936 that our fate was settled. At that moment we could with the minimum of risk have stopped the German revival in embryo, revised our faulty military ideas, and ensured a long period of peace. Later there was still time to build up our warlike stores, particularly after Munich, but the internal situation in France made this impossible.

Our reaction in March 1936 presupposed the existence of an adequate military instrument; but this we had not got. Palliatives were possible, as we have seen, but difficult. Thus it was in 1932–1934, when Germany, the occupation just over, was beginning her revival, that we should have reformed our own organization so that we would be in a position to strike at once if the need arose and then to bring ourselves up-to-date, particularly in armor and aviation. This would have required foresight, which indeed many had at the time—but foresight backed up by an energy which was lacking both in the high command and in the Government, which was too preoccupied with the present to bother about the future.

The lesson of this experience bears out the old saying "To govern is to foresee." Nothing is more destructive than a policy of "wait and see," which is always an excuse for doing nothing. The modern world, because of the time which economic and military plans nowadays take to realize, can no longer afford to think short-term. It is only by a constant reappraisal of the situation and an awareness of incipient dangers, that decisions can be taken in time to keep these future dangers in check. This is undoubtedly a condemnation of any political system which has no guarantee of continuity.

It remains to say something of the men who were involved. I have been particularly hard on Gamelin—the original choice of whom and his maintenance in command were both catastrophic—because he was in control during the decisive time when destiny might still have been turned aside. Instead he allowed an irredeemable situation to arise of which he himself was the first victim. Were there any others who might perhaps have done better? It is possible; but, as I have said, by 1940 it was really too late. In any case, it is not for me to play the dangerous and futile game of apportioning praise or blame in judgment on the leaders of this generation who, whatever their personal qualities, had been heavily scarred by the events which had taken place between the two wars.

This burden was above all the fruit of the long maturation imposed on the Army by the mental attitude of the victors of 1918. But it is difficult to avoid the conclusion that the pre-eminence of this doctrine may well have accorded with the thinking of most Frenchmen at the time.

One is then tempted to go a little further. Why was France, so ardent and resolute in 1914, this time so passive and lulled into taking the easy way out? The evident reason is the terrible exhaustion caused by the First World War which, at the same time, took every vestige of romance out of the test of battle. Patriotism, so firmly implanted in the French spirit, had lost much of its magic. Patriotism may have been in some respects ingenuous, but in recent times it assumed a somewhat tarnished image through the unintelligible contradictions of collaboration, the Resistance and the giving up of our colonies. A similar mental attitude was to be found in Germany after the disasters of 1945, and in this respect even Great Britain, which had suffered neither invasion nor defeat, was not spared.

The inescapable conclusion is that 1940 was but the last step in an inevitable progression. Destiny by certain fortuitous and extraordinary events, such as the command at Sedan losing its head and the accidental death of Billotte, showed clearly that we were lost. To use an expression which has become fashionable, we were swept away by the current of history. It is this feeling of inexorable fate which I have tried to describe. It is this which, like a Greek tragedy, dominated our whole dramatic downfall.

But the current of history is merely a synthesis of the natural turn of events to which whole peoples surrender themselves, and from which no one can escape unless he finds a means ,of constructive reaction. It is the role of great men to escape from the fate of history—or rather, to create another, counter-balancing, fate. Chance, which governs events, dictated that the one man in France who revealed the necessary stature came to the fore too late, when practically all was lost.

The war of 1914–1918, which destroyed so much, had nearly destroyed the myth of the great man. The appalling experience of 1940, with the bitter fruits of which we have not yet done, left in its wake one valuable lesson: mankind and nations are but the playthings of destiny if they cannot foresee mounting perils and rise up in time to combat them. This they cannot do unless they discover how to make ready the élite who can grasp the rudder firmly in any storm and can steer a safe course through treacherous waters.

John C. Cairns

THE MILITARY COLLAPSE WAS
EUROPEAN

*John C. Cairns (1924–   ) was born in Windsor, Ontario, received a Ph.D.
from Cornell University in 1951, and is currently Professor of History at the
University of Toronto. He is a specialist in Modern France, and his many
papers and articles have shed much light on the events of 1939–1940. He
has long been working on what promises to be one of the first comprehen-
sive studies on the fall of France. This selection brings out Professor Cairns'
keen awareness of the many facets and complexities of the question.*

The most famous army in the world may also have been the most
disparate, and Fortune or incapacity was to visit the heaviest shock
upon its worst-trained units. War of course would always be the
province of the unforeseen. History would note that the so-called
Manstein Plan, which finally brought the weight of enemy armor
down through the Ardennes to dislocate divisions of the Second
and Ninth Armies within days of the assault of May 10, came to
execution almost as the chance product of the Führer's intuitive
military mind. It might all have been so different. But it was not.
Lieut.-General Brooke of the Second Corps, B.E.F., reviewing a November parade beside the Ninth Army commander, General Corap—
destined to be the great military name publicly and unfairly branded
in the coming battle—stood appalled by the sight. "Seldom have I
seen anything more slovenly and badly turned out," he recalled.
"Men unshaven, horses ungroomed, clothes and saddlery that did
not fit, vehicles dirty, and complete lack of pride in themselves or
their units." "I could not help wondering," ran his diary entry that
night, "whether the French are still a firm enough nation to again
take their part in seeing this war through." The event showed that
these reserve divisions could not hold before the German fury.
Officers and men turned and fled. Corap bore the public odium for
a military concept that was as old as the great Revolution and as
outworn. "What happened to Corap could have happened to us

From John C. Cairns, "The Fall of France, 1940: Thoughts on a National Defeat,"
Proceedings of the Canadian Historical Association, 1957, pp. 58–63. Reprinted by
permission of Professor Cairns.

all," General Huntziger remarked during the battle, for disaster had brushed his Second Army also. A whole system had been condemned. All the complications at the top, the command divisions existing between Gamelin and Georges, the ill-considered entry into Belgium, the advent of Weygand, the conduct of Lord Gort, the vast disputed question of British cooperation by land and air—all these things merely served to underline the basic failure of the French military machine, so huge, so cumbrous, so utterly unfit to fight. Though fight part of it did, bravely, hopelessly, cut to pieces by an enemy who wheeled through the bright summer countryside and startled villages, past hundreds of thousands fleeing westward and south towards heaven knew what, unseeing, unbelieving, alternately panicked and dulled by the terrible spectacle of the great *déroute*.

Yet it was not so simple a thing as military leadership or discipline. "The word 'responsibility' is a very general term," General Georges reminded the Parliamentary commissioners long afterward. Weygand, as always, was explosive and more direct: "I must tell you that in the Army we are unanimous in thinking that the politicians want to place the whole responsibility for the defeat—I speak very plainly to you—on the military men. And that we will not accept." Certainly no observer could entirely disagree here and must stand perplexed before the spectacle of a civilian control which was scarcely exercised and a "responsible" Government which went largely unchecked, baffled by the welter of conflicting facts and figures on appropriations, equipment, matters of ordering and supply. This dreadful inquest on past responsibilities, begun even before the six-weeks war had come to its end, dragged itself out in the Riom Courthouse in a sad profusion of bitter recriminations to clear a people's uneasy conscience. Not the least unpleasant event of the Vichy regime, this debate (for it became a debate and not a trial) reflected little credit on soldiers or civilians. In a slightly less political manner it has continued to the present day, to the point where one felt an overwhelming compulsion to retire from the maddening task of achieving even an acceptable list of war materiel. Colonel Goutard's success in demonstrating that 1940 was another "war of lost opportunities" ought not to beguile History into easy assumptions about non-military roles. Senator Maroselli's account of his struggle to obtain an airing of the aircraft production problem before and during the war communicates something of the frustration he felt, faced by the "scandalously eloquent" facts he presented to the President of the Council. "It would be criminal to continue with this aviation policy which has brought us where we are," ran a letter of January 9, 1940: "we must end, quickly and decisively, this fatal policy pregnant with disaster." Previous representations had achieved nothing; this time there was not even a reply. A secret session in the Chamber one month later revealed an evasiveness and an ignorance in Parliament and the Ministry which merely foreshadowed coming events. The figures coming from the Tribune were misleading, not least because the Government appeared to have been misled by the air force or ministerial staff. The Minister for Air was publicly silenced by the President of the Council. The Deputies heard Daladier promise that they could contemplate an air war, whatever the inevitable losses, "with a certain assurance." And the sitting ended on a familiar note of harmony which showed that Robert de Jouvenel's *République des Camarades* was changeless as the Palais Bourbon.

The air force might have been the most sensational weakness; it was only one. How many matters of supply, of labor, of equipment, of organization could bear the light of investigation? Doubtless every nation at war had its problems of industrial bureaucracy, its multiplications and cancellings-out of offices. Doubtless the production troubles of France were reduced upon the creation of the Ministry of Armaments under Raoul Dautry shortly after the war began. Perhaps it was no more than bad luck that France suffered a catastrophe where other nations escaped because of time or geography. Yet one emerged from the labyrinth of disputed figures with the conviction that something fundamental had been wrong. It was not a mere matter of Hotchkiss tanks being manufactured with steering-mechanisms which failed after less than 300 kilometers, or of Bloch bombers which could not take off with full fuel and bomb load. Responsibilities at that level pointed inevitably upward, reaching always into the political arena where Parliamentary commissions had been too readily satisfied because of ignorance or indifference or politics; where Ministers had been misinformed or disinclined to answer questions and had taken refuge in appeals to patriotism, to confidence in the *grands chefs,* and to memories of other days and other trials which still in 1939–1940 cast their evening-glow of victory over a nation which now sought only the contemplation of this last. One could add the figures a dozen different ways: what they told was more or less the same; it was civil and military failure.

Still, the more one looked the more one became convinced that this Strange Defeat would never be comprehensible considered solely as a French phenomenon. The Armistice of June 25 was French, but the military collapse was European. Perhaps outside of France this had been too much lost sight of. It had come to seem inevitable that students should learn how Gamelin made no reply to his representative General Faury, August 22, 1939, when asked what the expectant Poles should be told; how Georges then spoke up to say that there was no knowing when the French Army would be able to attack; and how eventually Gamelin said simply: "Poland must hold out." But would they also learn how unprepared were France's allies? The valuable but somewhat sterilized pages of Major Ellis and Professor Butler might not really communicate the fantastic lack of preparation prevailing that year when the United Kingdom undertook to offer guarantees in Europe against aggression. Evidently official histories have their limitations as well as their uses. One looked elsewhere. The diary entries of General Brooke reflected more faithfully that underestimation of the enemy which characterized Lord Gort, the British Government, and possibly the people as a whole. For later condemnations of "the colossal military disaster which occurred when the French High Command failed to withdraw the Northern Armies from Belgium at the moment when they knew that the French front was decisively broken at Sedan and on the Meuse" were too easy and too late. The unfortunate Dyle maneuver with all its potential risks had been freely accepted the previous autumn, as Mr. Churchill himself admitted. Doubtless the tiny British land force of little more than ten divisions had discouraged serious questioning of the French plan, but one might doubt the intention itself. Whatever her sea and air effort, Great Britain was content to follow the French on foot. In the face of intransigent German bellicosity British policy before September had precipitated war; after September French policy precipitated defeat: ironic conclusion to more than thirty years of wavering entente. Were not the terrible events of the six-weeks' war only footnotes to the original errors? For it was not only the front that was broken in the crossing of the Meuse. An elaborate myth collapsed and disappeared not later than the summer day when a British General lost his temper and shook the commander of the French First Army Group by the button of his tunic to shock him back into action. The painful scenes and encounters between French and British along the refugee-packed roads and on the beaches and piers were an end to 1904 and all that. What Weygand called "twenty years of mutual suspicion and hesitation" closed as Brooke and his staff sailed around the Breton peninsula on June 18, "mostly lying on the deck in the sunshine and thanking God that we were safely out of France for the second time."

All this and more compelled examination if the events of 1940 were to make any sense. Unless the British role were evaluated fairly there could be no history above the level of national prejudice which—to take only the example of French judgments—had sometimes reduced this war to a case of British desertion and Belgian treason. In retrospect, there would seem to be something desperately sick and weak in the alacrity with which the surrender of May 28 was condemned and Leopold made the scapegoat for so many misfortunes. For the French, of course, allowances would be made. They had waited so long, been alerted so often, made so many representations to Brussels in vain, been given scarcely the slightest cooperation, and finally had staked all on reaching the river Dyle or even the Albert Canal to save not only themselves and the Belgian Army but what they could also of the land. All that only to see a King accept defeat and choose surrender rather than exile. The unleashing of French fury against him was a shocking action born of fear and frustration, but it was understandable then as the German armor moved up to Dunkirk to destroy the finest divisions of the French Army. Perhaps it was some sort of psychological identification which led them to condemn in others what they would so soon accept for themselves. Perhaps the French would afterwards comprehend the feelings of Leopold as he explained himself to his Ministers shortly after five in the morning, May 25, in the Château de Wynendaele, telling them why he could not leave, why his Armies were at their last gasp, predicting the proximate fall of France and the continuation of Great Britain's war, which could not then, however, help Belgium. At the time they did not understand. Yet a student would have to take account of it all, just as he would have to take account of the French reaction to it, if ever he were to make anything of the Strange Defeat.

And then, too, weighing the external factors, he could hardly neglect the enemy, his plans, strengths and weaknesses. For war in the West was something more than the rather gay and dashing Panzer thrusts of Generals Schmidt, Reinhardt and Guderian so breathtakingly recorded in the letters and diaries of Erwin Rommel. A long chain of events stretched from September to June; they were not all brilliant. Every account must make room for Hitler sitting silent after Paul Schmidt had translated the British ultimatum, deep in thought, immobile, then suddenly asking, "What now?" What of the many alarms, alerts, and doubts of the long cold winter? Or that awful January day two German officers crashed in Belgium carrying orders for an imminent invasion of the Low Countries, precipitating the Führer into what Field-Marshal Keitel later called "the nicest storm" he had ever witnessed and leading to an overhauling of German plans? Those who allowed themselves to be blinded by sentiment, ideology or the verve of the German success, the "sixty days that shook the West," to use Jacques Benoist-Méchin's title, would have to do their homework again. History would probably reject the view of a preordained outcome; everything would have to be weighed as often as fresh evidence came into view. "We never imagined war in the West would be like this," Rommel wrote to his wife. And four months before he was hanged at Nürnberg Keitel reminisced at length about the Dyle and Manstein maneuvers and the opportunities France and Britain had lost.

For us, of course, it is a matter less of pursuing didactic purposes than of seeking understanding. Since we are not pupils of Colonel Goutard, we do not feel the professional military urgency to explain away the enemy's victory: our lessons may be touched with a doubt and even a pessimism which is probably not acceptable in military schools. The indispensable thing must always be to try to see the possibilities and only then, if necessary, accept the apparent fatality of events. No account which did not place the hesitations and fears of the German Army beside the mistakes of the French and British would satisfy History. If it was true that the French entered the war with no plan of campaign, it was not less true that the Germans had none for the West. And though Clio must always be on the side of the successful she will remember that General von Brauchitsch once tendered his resignation rather than agree to the invasion of France. She will also remember, of course, that the resignation was refused and that within little more than six months Adolf Hitler stood looking down on Napoleon's tomb.

Pierre Cot
THE BREAKUP OF THE FRANCO-RUSSIAN ALLIANCE

A prolific writer on political and technical subjects, Pierre Cot (1895–   ) is closing out a long career on the faculty of the Ecole Pratique des Hautes Etudes. *He is best known, however, as an important political figure of the Third and Fourth Republics. Cot, who made his way to the United States after the fall of France, served as a Radical-Socialist Deputy from 1928 to 1940, and again, this time under the Progressist label, from 1946 to 1958. His tenure as Minister of the Air in Léon Blum's first Popular Front govern-ment (1936–1937) involved him directly in the stormy debate over the state of the French Air Force at the outbreak of the war. Pierre Cot here seeks to reduce the question to its proper dimensions.*

I was Minister of the Air for 18 or 19 months. This is too short a period to reap what one has sown. It takes much longer to build factories and to start production of new aircraft. If you want to measure the effectiveness of the reforms initiated in 1936–1937, you should not consider the production figures of 1937, or even 1938, but those of 1939. As I have already stated, at the outbreak of the war, our rate of production was five times that of June 1936. . . .

By relaxing the tensions between employers and workers, the

From *Les Evénements survenus en France de 1933 à 1945, Témoignages et documents recueillis par la Commission d'Enquête Parlementaire, Rapport—Annexes (Dépositions)* (Paris: Presses Universitaires de France, 1947), I, pp. 283; 284; 285–286. Reprinted by permission of the Secretary General of the National Assembly of France. [Editor's translation.]

nationalization of the aircraft industry facilitated the settlement of social problems. When I assumed office in June 1936, labor-management relations had so far deteriorated that all factories were shut by sit-down strikes. Such was the situation I inherited from Marcel Déat, my immediate predecessor. A few days later, agreement was reached on a new contract through collective bargaining, and work resumed everywhere. Not a single day's labor was lost through strikes in the nationalized factories during the whole of my tenure at the Ministry of the Air. There were two short strikes in the private sector of the industry: one at the Renault plant in Paris, the other at the Latécoère plant in Toulouse. They were promptly settled by arbitration. I might add that in both cases the decision was against the employers.

I would not want to create the impression that we did not face great difficulties, or that the nationalization of the aircraft industry took place smoothly. Far from it! We had to overcome tremendous obstacles. Some manufacturers, who had retained possession of their plants and opposed nationalization, systematically tried to sabotage the whole program. The banks often refused to grant us the credits needed to operate the nationalized plants. The suppliers of raw materials slowed down production by failing to meet the delivery deadlines specified in their contracts. This was especially true of aluminum and special parts manufacturers. We thus had to wage a constant battle against the ill will of some, the impatience of others, and the political prejudice or just plain stupidity of many. I would like to pay tribute, however, to the workers, the technicians, and to those industrialists who deserved well of the country by participating wholeheartedly in the program I was trying to launch. To be sure, there were conscious and unintentional saboteurs. But there were many, many more men of good will and honest workers at every level of the hierarchy. All industrialists did not act like M. Renault. . . .

Should you think that we might have done more before the war, please keep two things in mind. First, as I have already pointed out, between 1936 and 1939, our industrial capacity was one-third of Germany's. Second, there was the financial factor. From June 1936 to September 1939 we allocated some 750 million dollars for the expansion of our air force. During the same period, England spent

1,600 million dollars (roughly twice the amount), and Germany 3,000 million dollars (nearly five times as much). The top English and German military leaders had been able to grasp the importance of air power in modern war much better and sooner than our own. That will be the verdict of history. All other commentaries are but prattling inspired by political prejudice. . . .

We lost the war, or rather the battle of 1940, for political rather than technical reasons. A brief comparison of prewar conditions in 1914 and 1939 will prove the validity of this statement.

Why did we avoid defeat in 1914? Because our Ministers of National Defense and military leaders had shown more foresight than they did during the interwar period? Because we had better prepared for war militarily and technically? You know as well as I do that this was not the case. In 1939, we had a shortage of planes and tanks; in 1914, we did not have enough heavy artillery and machine guns. What, then, was the basic difference between 1914 and 1939?

The basic difference is that, in 1914, we were allied with both England and Russia. Without the Russian advance in East Prussia, we would never have been able to rally at the Marne. In 1939, we did not have the support of Soviet Russia. Nothing can obscure this fact. Suppose that we had had a few hundred more planes. It would not have mattered in the least. We were not defeated because we were short some three or four hundred planes. After all, we still had more than a thousand aircraft at the ready after the Armistice. Suppose, on the other hand, that the Soviet Union had come to our help. Germany would then have been unable to hurl her whole might against us, and the shape of things would have been altered. Need I remind you that the Red Army of 1939 was more powerful, better equipped, better led, and had a higher morale than the Tsarist Army of 1914? Further, the Russian industrial capacity was ten times what it had been in 1914.

Think this over, and ask yourselves whether we did everything in our power, before and after Munich, to secure the help of the Red Army and the Soviet Union. At any rate, no one will deny that this witness worked tirelessly to that end.

Historians, some day, will come to the conclusion that France lost the battle of 1940 because she did not have the support of the Soviet Union. To prove the point, they will have only to advance comparative statistics on the industrial capacity of the contending parties. The military effectives of the most courageous nation—and the resistance movement was to show that the French people did not lack courage—cannot possibly exceed its industrial potential.

The primary cause for our defeat having been established, you might want to consider some of the contributing factors. Ask yourselves, then, whether we might not have allocated a larger part of our national defense budget to the development of the air force. Ask yourselves who was guilty of lack of foresight: the civilians who constantly asked that air power be assigned a greater role in the overall schemes of national defense, or the conservative and routine-minded soldiers who declared, in 1937, that there was no need to expand the air force?

Finally, to get down to cases, you might want to know why we were unable to produce more planes. Ask yourselves, then, whether those ministers who were able to prevent strikes and to ease social tensions, did not serve the country better than those financiers and industrialists who paralyzed their initiatives, and sometimes crippled their programs, by a concerted opposition to the laws passed by Parliament?

I was condemned, or at least censured, by Marshal Pétain's Council of Political Justice. But as I look back on my career, there are two other judgments that I would like to invoke. The first is that of the Spanish Republicans, whom I tried to help as best I could. The second is Hitler's accusation, at the time of Munich, that I had tried to foment a Czecho-Soviet alliance against Nazi Germany. Gentlemen, a man who has been condemned by Pétain, attacked by Hitler, and lauded by the enemies of Fascism, has a clear conscience.

IV THE INTELLECTUAL, SOCIAL, AND PSYCHOLOGICAL FACTORS

Pierre Drieu La Rochelle
RATIONALISM: *VOILA L'ENNEMI!*

Like many gifted French writers of the interwar period, Pierre Drieu La Rochelle (1893–1945) came to despair of democratic institutions. A strong supporter of Jacques Doriot's neo-fascist Parti Populaire Français during the late 1930s, he became director of the Nouvelle Revue Française and an advocate of out-and-out collaboration with Nazi Germany during the Occupation. Deeply compromised, Drieu La Rochelle committed suicide rather than face arrest and trial after the Liberation. The following sample of his writings at once offers a highly intellectual explanation for the debacle, and delineates the depth and bitterness of French quarrels.

France was destroyed by the rationalism to which her genius had been reduced. Today, rationalism is dead and buried. We can only rejoice at its demise. The destruction of the monster that had been gnawing away at the very soul of France was the *sine qua non* of her revival. The French people were too far gone to cure themselves of the disease. We can only rejoice when we think that the unchecked influence of rationalism might eventually have corrupted the true values of life, passion, and reason throughout Europe and the whole world.

France had lost body and soul. Only a small mechanism, wound up one last time, held her together. The whole mechanism broke down at the first shock. Through ignorance, stupidity, or habit, some Frenchmen continued to believe in the effectiveness of the mechanism. Others tried, as best they could, to free France and to steer her toward the mainstream of the European Revolution. The latter had to wage an uphill fight. On the one hand, the late occurrence of the Russian experiment provided French rationalism with enough new evasive arguments to permit it to linger on. On the other, pride, and misguided patriotic inhibitions prevented the French mind from adapting itself to the new spirit abroad in Europe.

The France of the scouts, hikers, and skiers was not strong enough to overcome the France of the idlers, Pernod drinkers, river-

From Pierre Drieu La Rochelle, *Notes pour compréndre le siècle* (Paris, 1941), pp. 171–175. Copyright © 1941 by Editions Gallimârd. Reprinted by permission. [Editor's translation.]

bank fishermen, and the salon, committee, and syndicate babblers. The France of the determined militants of the Extreme-Right and the Extreme-Left was not strong enough to overcome the France of the prattling conservatives, who shamelessly continued to call themselves moderates, radicals, or socialists.

The France that had read Sorel, Barrès, Maurras, Péguy, Bernanos, Céline, Giono, Malraux, Petitjean was not strong enough to overcome the France that had read Anatole France, Duhamel, Giraudoux, Mauriac, Maurois.

The France of Morocco and Indochina, of the aviators and missionaries was not strong enough to overcome the France of the stay-at-home, the card players, and the bowlers.

The decaying effect of Freemasonry was apparent everywhere. Administrator-Bishops spewed a viler brand of rationalism than the Sorbonne professors under the misleading label of "Thomism," or muttered old maidish incantations to the Sacred Heart or Saint Joseph. The Legion of Honor had two hundred thousand "members." Funeral establishments like the *Ecole Normale, Polytechnique, Inspection des Finances, Conseil d'Etat, Quai d'Orsay,* etc., caused the premature intellectual death of our youth. The nonconformism affected by the civil servants and the schoolteachers was but an envious aping of the conformism of their betters. The press consisted of illiterate millionaires surrounded by humiliated lackeys. Literature had its academies for spineless writers, its hundred thousand Prizes, and its dull reviews (including the *Nouvelle Revue Française,* which aged more rapidly than the *Revue des Deux Mondes* or the *Revue de Paris* during the preceding century, and which stood somewhere between the fringe of surrealism and the pedantry of the war horses of rationalism). The nobility had become indistinguishable from the middle class and mistook insipidity for good manners. The bourgeoisie had stifled what vitality it had left by trying to emulate the titled middle class. The Jews were bent on promoting every possible form of corruption in the mistaken and cowardly belief that this was the only path to security. The lower bourgeoisie divided its time between movie houses and cafés. The workers had become more bourgeois than the bourgeoisie, and their sole social concern was the fluctuation of the wage scale. Their antifascism was no more fervent than the anticommunism of the bourgeoisie. While congenitally incapable of becoming either fascists or communists, they were ready to applaud a comic opera Russia from afar. They refused to act like patriots at Moscow's command, but they were quite capable of becoming defeatists and debunkers at the first signal from the same direction. The peasants were ashamed of their calling, and their sole concern was to accumulate savings. All this was France, and France amounted to no more than this.

Jean Dutourd

THE LOST GENERATION

After a brief experience as a private during the last stages of the Battle of France and active participation in a Parisian Resistance group, Jean Dutourd (1920–   ) emerged from World War II "an angry young man." His The Best Butter, *a highly amusing but devastating commentary on black-market operations during the Occupation, first brought Dutourd to the attention of the English-speaking world. Bitter wit and mordant satire have indeed characterized the best work of this talented and versatile writer. In* The Taxis of the Marne, *from which the following selection is taken, these traits are somewhat tempered by a deep love of country. Yet, Dutourd's indictment of "the men of fifty" is utterly merciless.*

On the 25th June 1940, at the age of twenty years and six months, after having been a soldier for fourteen days, I was taken prisoner. I have no bad memories of this experience. After twenty years of childhood, school and university, it made a change. For a week I marched across Brittany in the company of four other soldiers of my unit and an Alsatian sergeant of the name of Joseph, called Cepi. We wanted to steal a dinghy in some small port and coast down to Bordeaux. We were very keen on this plan. As for me, I was so proud of my uniform that for nothing in the world would I have left it in a ditch. To keep it, I believe, seemed to me all the more important since we had been defeated. All six of us were luxuriating in

From Jean Dutourd, *The Taxis of the Marne,* tr. Harold King (London, 1957), pp. 13–17; 135–139; 143–147. Copyright © 1957 by Jean Dutourd. Reprinted by permission of Simon and Schuster, Inc., and Martin Secker & Warburg Limited.

friendship. The population helped and protected us. In one inn, a pretty girl served me beef stew with a great deal of tenderness. I was only twenty; this tenderness pleased me and I did not think of taking advantage of it. Or rather, I did think of it, but I did not do it.

Our gang was very gay. We were no longer quite soldiers, but we had kept our arms and steel helmets. Each of us had a revolver which we might perhaps have made use of on occasion. Crossing Brittany on foot, seeing the disorganization in the region, the flight of the population, the stampede of the authorities, and even the rout of inanimate things (we saw mattresses abandoned in open fields, which is not where mattresses belong), I thought that France was strained like a rope and that the rope must slacken or break. I remember making the comparison: it was running round in my head during the whole of my journey. The rope slackened to the great relief of everybody when Pétain announced on the wireless that he had asked for an armistice.

What would have happened if the rope had snapped? I did not dare imagine. That France could burst like a soap bubble passed my understanding. Not only was I young and without experience, but I was also suffering from that natural defect of youth, timidity; I could not bring myself to conceive of a complete overthrow and a total destruction. In truth, we were lacking in desperation. What we should have had was the desperation of Finland. We were not up to the militiamen of the Army of the Loire or to the Federates.

In certain circumstances a man must be ready to die on the spot. I did not know this. Cepi, who was a commercial traveller or something like it in civilian life, was also ignorant of this, and in any case he did not have the qualities essential in a leader. He was a decent fellow, not stupid and quite resourceful, who soon put us at our ease by telling us: "No need to call me sergeant any more. We are all equal now. Call me Cepi." As he was seven or eight years older than us, he believed it was his duty to save the lives of my four companions and myself. Which incidentally he did. He led us to Auray, where we were all six taken prisoner without a scratch.

Duty obviously demanded that we should stop in some village, build a barricade and fire on the first German motorcyclists that turned up. Five stalwarts in every village of Brittany, and the face of the war would have been changed. This was evidently not the "Brittany redoubt," but what of it? We should have held the Morbihan, the Finistère, and the Côtes du Nord for a week. In a week, an army corps could have been reconstituted somewhere and could have been sent to the rescue. And even if no army corps had come, that week would have been worth living. Not all of us would have died, and honor would have been saved. The recruits of Brittany who had only had two weeks of training would have had the pleasure of being called "the flower of French youth." In 1940 the French had not astonished the world for a long time. But nobody thought of such a thing. And I, who am moralizing here and amusing myself at rewriting history, did not think of it either until two or three years later.

Courage, like artistic inspiration, begets itself. It is not very difficult to act courageously when you have already done it once, just as it is easier to write the hundredth page of a book than the first. In June 1940 I was not courageous, but I would have become so with the greatest of ease. It would have been enough to have been courageous once. If Sergeant Cepi had led us into danger instead of skillfully leading us away from it, we should quite naturally have become heroes.

Apparently the hour for courage had not struck. France had forgotten the word. The government had even lost our traditions of martial eloquence. Shades of Danton and Gambetta! All they could think of to galvanize us was the propaganda slogan: "We shall win because we are the strongest."

Base words, the exhortation of a mean government to a cowardly people. They ought to have painted on the walls in enormous letters: "We shall win because we are the bravest." Was the government afraid that if it talked of bravery the country would laugh in its face? Certainly, it can happen to be *crushed* by an enemy very superior in numbers or in equipment, but this was not our case. On the contrary. We were in fact the strongest. If God is on the side of the big battalions, he was on our side, and all the more so as the enemy was not worth anything. Our fathers, the *poilus*, who pulverized the redoubtable army of the Kaiser, would have made short work of those young Nazi guttersnipes trembling in their cardboard fortlets. All our big battalions lacked was courage, the courage about which nobody whispered a word as if it were some shameful disease. On September

3, 1939, the war was not lost. It was lost in the months that followed, and search as I would, I can find only one reason for our defeat: stupidity and cowardice. The generals were stupid, the men did not want to get killed. These two things often go together. Troops know that an idiot has no right to ask them to get killed. We were the strongest and we did not conquer. Virtue was missing.

The French generals had the instrument of victory in their hands, but what nobody realized was this: they were longing to change their profession. They did not like war. They had mistaken their vocation. As another soldier, their spiritual father, guessed so well, their real inclination was for quieter occupations: accountant, postmaster, colonial administrator, lawyer, prefect, police commissioner, high court judge; in other words, they secretly longed to be civil servants. No more army, for the love of Heaven! *No more responsibilities!*

I feel a personal grudge against these peace-loving generals. Mistaking their own vocation, they sabotaged mine. When I look at myself today, I burst with rage, I who am thrilled by the slightest flourish of trumpets, who get tears in my eyes when I read "Honneur et Fidélité," who become breathless at the thought of the wooden hand of Captain Danjou, who am bowled over by the statue of Marshal Ney holding out his sword near the site of the old "Bal Bullier," who am transfixed by the *Marseillaise* of Rude and overcome by the flame under the Arc de Triomphe. If those sorry men had not broken my career in June 1940, I would be a knight of the Legion of Honor (a Legion of Honor worth wearing), I would have been it at the age of twenty and a captain in the finest infantry in the world. Curse the damnable scoundrels!

. . . My contemporaries sometimes tell me that our youth was ruined and that those who were twenty in 1940 were a sacrificed generation. The war, captivity, the occupation, the crises, and the afflictions of the period robbed us of seven or eight years during which we just kept body and soul together on empty stomachs and raging hearts. All that is true, but I can never see how my youth was ruined by it. It was a hard youth, no doubt, poverty-stricken and dangerous, but exhilarating; it was a youth of warriors and conspirators which in the end enriched me much more than would have a glittering youth dissipated in amorous adventures and social successes.

There are various ways of accomplishing one's sentimental education. The way of Flaubert's Frédéric Moreau has always filled me with disgust. Yet that represents what today is called "gilded youth." Frédéric Moreau *had a good time.* He had an income of his own; he was in with the right set; he had love affairs and spent money freely; he tasted debauchery—in short, he "lived," he "sucked the orange dry."

What a futile way of living it is, this supposedly "real life," recalled afterwards in middle age with satisfaction and vain regrets. "When you have really lived, you will understand that. . . ." How many times this sentence was inflicted upon me. It was all I heard between the age of fifteen and twenty-five, pronounced in a self-satisfied voice by dozens of incompetents or imbeciles. Having "really lived" amounts to a few follies one regrets, a few women one did not understand how to love, a few companions with whom one was bored, a few hopes abandoned. There is, in truth, a lesson in this: how small must be the heart such poor things suffice to fill.

The French reserve officers who were thirty or forty in 1940 were almost all men whose youth resembled that of Frédéric Moreau. Ladies of easy virtue and pleasure do not corrupt strong souls, but the souls of the young middle-class Frenchmen of that time must have been less firmly anchored than those of their ancestors, since when the war came they were irretrievably lost and incapable of displaying any virtue whatsoever. Compared with those timorous officers, anxious to preserve their pleasant existence and their belongings, the German officers who had lived through ten years of hardship followed by ten other years of tyranny seemed like men of iron. I do not mean that Spartan discipline is worth more than Athenian refinement. I am simply noting that France's gentle art of living, the celebrated *douceur de la vie,* does not agree with everybody. Some generations favored by nature stand it very well and find in happiness the strength to defend it; others, less energetic, discover to their cost that it engenders nothing but fattened-up rabbits whose fate it is to be gobbled up as rabbit-pie.

The men of fifty, born around 1900 or soon after, are far more tragic "offsprings of the century" than were the contemporaries of Musset and Vigny a century earlier. Feeling poor blood flowing in their veins, seeing around them the ruins of a country and a civilization they had found powerful and allowed to be destroyed, they too could exclaim not in anger but in despair: "I came too late into a world too old." Like the men born in 1800, they too had a prodigious childhood, with fathers steeped in the blood of the enemy, with the spectacle before them of a warlike and victorious nation. It is hard to remember today the glory and force of France between 1918 and 1938. They were so great that her children asked themselves no questions. They were children who were too rich, who looked upon their happiness with a pout of disdain. The Great War that our generals won so ferociously, seeing whole divisions perish without batting an eyelid, only left these children with an indigestion of patriotism. As war veterans, their fathers, the heroes, soon began to bore them. For four years the rear from which these adolescents watched these massacres had sickened them with its abject boasting that managed to make the most respectable things and men look ridiculous. Everything on this subject has already been said. What has not been mentioned is the distant and pernicious influence this bluff and eyewash had on the youth of the time, and the tremendous reaction of scepticism and contempt that the jingoism of the civilians provoked. Scepticism and contempt are nearly always without limit. After the men of the 1922 age-group had got over their childhood enthusiasms and made the acquaintance of sergeant instructors who had spent the whole war in Toulouse, they started loathing their idols and set to work demolishing them.

The *poilus* of 1914 were fathers whom their sons found too heavy to bear. They had too much glory, and too much official glory. There was nothing left for anyone else. They were ceaselessly held up for admiration. They offered themselves as examples, reflecting the characteristic mark of our modern political systems based on public opinion, which mark is propaganda, that is to say, boastfulness. How was it possible for anybody with any pride not to revolt against these all-pervading fathers, however great their merits had been? Moreover, after peace was signed, the war veterans provided the world with distressing demonstrations of a successful army grown old and commemorating its own victories. When they swapped their steel-helmets for berets, the war veterans stepped down from epic stature to provincial pettiness. They "hung on." Did they really think their mass parades in some way fashioned the policy of France?

They probably did, but they were mistaken; heroes are not suffered gladly. For ten or fifteen years, these heroes and their ineffectual complaints met with more or less willing consideration, but after that they became open figures of fun. Their leaders died off and they themselves became peevish old fogies. The whole thing ended in making a little ridiculous and tame a very great adventure which will perhaps stand in history as the last act of a victorious and powerful France.

The Great War appalled France and left her aghast. She had gone to the uttermost limits of effort; she almost died of it. The mad rejoicing over the victory did not alter the fact that she had been seized with horror. That war had nothing in common with preceding wars, not even the war of 1870, nor even with the last campaign of Napoleon. It was a foul war of troglodytes, Martians, and flying men. In 1914, the god Mars had suddenly become a gigantic juggernaut. Beside him, Jupiter no longer existed. Mars had sat down on Olympus and crushed it.

It is true, as a matter of fact, that in the words of the famous phrase there is something fresh and joyful about war, at any rate in its early days (for it is not without attraction for a man who is young and brave to go forth to measure himself against other men), and also in its final days when the victor is elated by his victory and his power. "Ah, God, how sweet is war, with its songs, with its prolonged leisures," wrote Apollinaire, who knew what he was writing about and had no resemblance whatever to the vile propagandists of the *Echo de Paris* of 1916. But the war was only fresh and joyful for one or two days while the men called to the colors were marching past in their red trousers and the girls stuck flowers in the barrels of their rifles. The following week these vigorous and cheerful boys of 1914, with their beautiful moustaches and pommaded hair, were already dying dirtily in the midst of the cherry orchards. They were going to die like that for four years, and more dirtily still: in filth and mud, tightening their bowels, squatting in trenches, crumpling up under the bombs and shells, suffocating with the obsessing smell of blood and excrement, cutting an enemy's throat with a knife, capturing machine-gun nests at the point of the bayonet, hurling back unexploded German hand-grenades, and still finding some way, even with a broken head and a gaping belly, to defend their country.

... Ah, you men of fifty, how you jeered at the war stories told by your fathers when you were twenty, still hot from their battles! How they forced them down your throats, their feats of valor, their wise-cracks, their jokes between two shells, their luck with the girls in the front-line villages, their memories of horror in the fox-holes, the cries of their dying friends, their little heroic wangles. You looked with pity on those poor old fellows. How on earth could anyone be a *poilu*? The peace of 1925, shining with a thousand lights, the Exhibition of Decorative Arts, the Charleston, steel furniture: these realities of life pushed such tedious epics into the shadows of the past. War veterans were bores whom the war had thrown off balance; they remained haunted by its horrors and pervaded by its memories. They never wanted to see that again and they did not want their children ever to see the like of it, but they could not hide their pride in it. This sanguinary and sordid story had been the great adventure of their lives. All right, they were a lot of old bores. But here's the rub, you men of fifty: you yourselves are now wearying our ears with your own stories. You have become a new lot of old bores. But your stories are tales of captivity. Thanks to your kind confidences, we know all about the five years during which you waited for the English, the Americans, the Russians, and a few Frenchmen (mostly of my generation and not of yours) to come and liberate you. We know you were gifted for the theater and that you showed talent in putting on boulevard comedies in the *Oflags*. We know you used your leisure in order to improve your minds, that the most knowledgeable amongst you gave interesting lectures, that the more audacious manufactured crystal sets, that you went in for painting watercolors, and that you won at backgammon the battles you lost on the battle-field. How you, in your turn, have forced your adventures down our throats. How well we know them. But they are pitiful adventures. Is it not true that your greatest hardship was to have been deprived of the company of women for eighteen hundred successive nights? What a trial for the former young dandies of 1925! After you got back, men of fifty, you pushed your aberration to the point of wearing a badge of barbed wire in your button-hole. You promoted this symbol of your shame to the rank of a military decoration. You formed associations of former prisoners of war. I must say that between "former prisoners of war" and "former soldiers," I choose the former soldiers. I prefer them. Tales of war bore me less than tales of captivity.

Naturally, there were honorable prisoners, but it is impossible in a national catastrophe to take special cases into account. It is the general impression that counts, and it is a terrible one. Supposing that out of one and a half million French prisoners two hundred thousand did not surrender without fighting: that leaves thirteen hundred thousand sheep. This crushing majority gives the event its true character. The two hundred thousand men are lost, smothered, they disappear beneath the thirteen hundred thousand unhappy men to whom danger taught no greatness of soul.

A very convenient confusion has been established between the hero and the martyr. There is nevertheless a difference: that between the positive and the negative; the hero acts, the martyr endures. Yes, you were martyrs, you men of fifty, but unintentionally. Your sin was to settle down to this martyrdom, to make yourself comfortable in it. Your crime was never to have despaired. I remember at the Arsenal hearing the theoreticians of captivity argue, while lapping up in their mess-tins the greasy water which constituted their entire lunch, that the only rational thing to do in a war was to get taken prisoner as soon as possible in order to be able to sit out the hostilities in peace and quiet. You remained prisoners of war for five years: you would just as well have remained there twenty years; you would have been prepared to spend the rest of your lives in the camps. Only the first year is painful. Little by little the system would have improved, discipline would have slackened. I am convinced that many prisoners left their camps with regret, and that today, faced with the high cost of living, taxation, business responsibilities, and the nagging of their wives, faced, in short, with the horrors of peace, they sigh and say: "Those were the days."

France, this aged unhappy mother, this pauper to whose rags still cling tattered bits of the fineries of the past: the frayed fleurs-de-lis, the tarnished eagles, the plucked cock; this parent you have forced to go begging at all the gates of the world, who is being kicked out of Africa and Asia, who is being spat in the face by the guttersnipes of Cairo, whose last resources are dropping from her rheumaticky hands; France will one day drag you, men of fifty, before the bar of history. She will point you out to your contemptuous and penniless posterity as the men guilty of her misfortunes and of the slavery into which she is already tottering. You thrust France into a paralytic's chair which we, your sons, must push. The lost generation is not our generation, it is yours. It was lost for everybody. The nation could have done without you. You cannot even dream of how poor you will be in a few years' time. Flourishing men of fifty, you will long ago have sold your automobiles, you will be famished and tired greybeards, having nothing to do in your unheated apartments but to chew over petty regrets for a happy defeat. It has repeatedly been said that France was betrayed in 1940. Of course she was betrayed. But not by the Fifth Column. She was betrayed by you, men of fifty. She was betrayed by what should have been her vital forces.

Alexander Werth
THE ROAD TO VICHY

A veteran newspaperman, Alexander Werth (1901–   ) served as the Paris correspondent of the Manchester Guardian *from 1931–1940. His many books and articles, which represent the very best in political reporting, are required reading for anyone seeking to understand domestic developments in France during this period. The fact that Werth was anything but sympathetic to the aspirations and politics of the French ruling classes lends special validity to his balanced verdict of their role and responsibilities in the events of 1939–1940. The reader should note that this selection is taken from a book published in 1942. Werth's later writings on the subject were somewhat less dispassionate.*

There is the purely military story; but I am not a military expert; and to the layman in Paris only the following points were clear:

1. In the Low Countries, the Allies were overwhelmed by the force of the German onslaught and the novelty of the German technique; above all, by the number of their tanks and their almost complete command of the air. France's 3,500 tanks were scattered all

From Alexander Werth, *The Twilight of France: 1933–1940* (New York & London, 1942), pp. 352–356. Copyright 1942 by Harper & Brothers. Reprinted by permission of Harper & Row, Publishers, and Hamish Hamilton Ltd.

over the front, and were never effectively used for any counter-offensive.

2. The lessons of the campaign in Poland, which was a first application of these principles, had been ignored and neglected on the easy assumption that the Poles are Poles and the French are French. Actually, everything tends to show that as an individual soldier the Pole was superior to the Frenchman.

3. While there were some remarkable cases of French resistance —notably at Rethel and at a few other more or less isolated points during the great German drive from the Meuse to the Channel Ports and also at Dunkirk, and a week later on the Somme—the general level of French morale was considerably lower than in 1914 when Germany at first also enjoyed an indisputable superiority in equipment.

4. Both the morale and efficiency of the French officers were, again, unequal to 1914–1918; and human life, generally, was prized too highly both by the French command *("avares du sang français")* and by many of the individuals directly concerned. I am merely stating a moral factor in France's collapse; I am not, as a civilian, presuming to criticize men each of whom faced far greater dangers and hardships than any of us civilians ever did; but the fact remains that, in many cases, the old spirit of Verdun was lacking. And the same is true of the women. They wept too much from the very day the Germans invaded Holland and Belgium.

5. Was there "Fifth Column" activity in the Army? There is no doubt that the Germans had numerous agents; and that bogus telephone calls, for instance, played a certain part in the disorganization of the French. But whether there were many officers and men who were consciously handing their country over to Germany is something about which I have no evidence; and I doubt whether plain treason played any great part in the German advance. But discouragement and—in the later stages of the war—the belief that the struggle was hopeless, and that if France was to survive she must "accommodate" herself to her defeat, were important factors, which largely account for the subsequent attitude at Bordeaux of men like Pétain and Weygand.

6. Lastly, it is clear that the real trouble, psychological and material, arose from the sudden collapse of the "Maginot" system on

which the whole organization of the French Army had been based, and which every French—and British—citizen had been taught to trust implicitly. The French had had the miracle of the Maginot Line drummed into them for years; perhaps it was lucky, from the point of view of morale, that the British soldier had heard of Maginot only a few months earlier, and also knew from direct experience when he arrived in the north of France earlier in the war that there was really nothing in the way of fortifications worth writing home about. The fortifications built by the British between the Channel, and, roughly, Hazebrouck, were in fact never attacked, but turned. The Germans broke through the French sector of the "extension"; and this had been the subject of the most deplorable and irresponsible optimism.

The decision not to defend Paris has often been criticized. I have no opinion on the question whether a successful defense of Paris was militarily possible; what evidence there is suggests that it was not. But there was the same psychological element in the decision not to defend Paris as in the formula *"avares du sang français."* Even a conquered France was better than a physically annihilated France; France might, in time, emancipate herself if her people were allowed to live on and rear children; and Paris might still be Paris provided it was not razed to the ground. To put it a little crudely: the old slogan of the Jacobins, *"Liberté ou la mort,"* had been abandoned for *"Esclavage—plus ou moins provisoire—plutôt que la mort,"* on the ground that what was most important to save, if anything could yet be saved, were the seeds of national, or rather, racial survival. In all this, there was a vague conception of "regeneration through suffering," and there was the strangely Chinese-like belief that "France could not be destroyed." There was also a tendency to take a very long, and very philosophical view of the whole thing: the French, as men of a higher civilization, would eventually absorb and convert the German conquerors; and pleasant parallels from history—how the Franks were civilized by the Gallo-Romans and how in the twelfth century the Kingdom of France was reduced to a tiny bit of country round Paris—appealed to many minds in these moments of distress. Already for a few years—particularly after Munich—writers like M. Detoeuf had liked to play about with such ideas of the inevitable regeneration of France through conquest and humiliation. Others, like Marcel Déat, went much further, and were, in effect, prepared to make the best of a bad situation by accepting wholeheartedly the New Order of Hitler and Mussolini, and by begging the supermen for a little place—oh, quite a little place—in the new scheme of things.

The motives that prompted the Bordeaux Government to surrender to Germany are, in fact, numerous and very mixed. The motif of expiation and renovation through suffering was present in some minds—and this perhaps was the most respectable of the motives. Others were prompted, either by cowardice or by what they believed to be their self-interest, to bow to the German demands, in the hope that the Germans would allow these people to become, as it were, the ruling caste in France—a caste which could now wreak vengeance on its political opponents. On the soil of defeat and disaster the seeds of Vichy had rapidly developed into a great monstrous flower. Here was something of all the things that one had already seen sprouting, especially since 1934. The 6th of February spirit; the anti-liberal and anti-parliamentary spirit, which was not merely critical of the abuses of the French parliamentary system, but absolutely hostile to the parliamentary, democratic idea; the cultivation of the peasantry—that good French peasantry which had already supported Napoleon III through thick and thin, as against the turbulent industrial proletariat; the shouts of *La France aux Français* which had in the heyday of the Croix de Feu and Jeunesses Patriotes and Solidarité Française resounded up and down the Champs-Elysées; the Nazi-inspired anti-semitism of *Gringoire* and *Je Suis Partout;* and the more authentically French anti-semitism of the *Action française;* the anti-Freemasonry of the old Stavisky days; and, above all, the anti-British explosions of *Gringoire* and the anti-British sentiments of many of the ordinary people, and also of the Lavals, the Bonnets, the Déats, the Paul Faures.

It was all there; the feeling that the British were selfish imperialists, who were ready to fight to the last French soldier; that the British had not sent enough troops and had let the French down. And even as late as the 16th and 17th of June, the men of Bordeaux were still full of pernicious illusions about Italy and Spain; even though Italy had declared war on France, and General Franco had converted his neutrality into nonbelligerency. The Latin bloc—the bloc of the Latin Nations, which would, in the long run, offset and cancel out Germany's hegemony on the Continent—this Latin bloc was still a favorite idea with Laval and Baudouin, and the aged Marshal Pétain. Daladier had sent him to Spain as French Ambassador in 'March 1939; he had allowed himself to be flattered and blackmailed by the Spaniards, and was ultimately persuaded by them that Hitler would offer him, the "Hero of Verdun," an honorable soldier's peace.

Was it possible for France to continue the war after the fall of Paris? The answer is yes, provided France was in a truly heroic mood. It would have meant grim sacrifices and fearful risks. In Weygand's view there was no line in European France which could be held successfully for any length of time. All the great industrial centers had fallen, or were about to fall, into the hands of the Germans. The only chance was to continue the war in North Africa. What did that mean? It meant first, that European France would be left entirely in the hands of Germany; and what fearful blackmail could the Germans not exercise on the Government of North Africa and the soldiers and sailors there? Anything from the massacre of the two million war prisoners to the massacre of the entire French population. Was such German blackmail—though perfectly compatible with the Nazi character—ever attempted? I do not know; but it is characteristic that stories of such blackmail should have been current at *Bordeaux* during the few days that preceded the armistice. The continuation of the war in North Africa would have been perfectly feasible; but it meant two things, both of which were distasteful to the men around Pétain; *it would have meant the perpetuation of the alliance with "democratic" England, and it would have meant that the war would be primarily fought against Italy.* And even the idea of a *revanche* on Germany *through the (relatively easy) defeat of Mussolini's Italy* was intolerable to the Lavals, the Pétains, the Ybarnégarays, the Baudouins, the De Monzies, and the rest who had, for years, been longing for Italy's friendship, and had been day-dreaming of the Latin bloc. Their political ideal was precisely Mussolini's Italy. These pernicious illusions were encouraged by the astonishingly mild armistice terms presented by the "victorious" Italians to France, and, later, by the lack of haste they showed in enforcing them.

There was a variety of motives behind the French decision to surrender. But whatever the different motives, all the men round Pétain shared, more or less, in the illusion that by surrendering to Hitler and by being polite and humble to Italy, they could build up a France of their own; that authoritarian *bien-pensant* capitalist and small-freeholder France in which they would rule under the more or less benevolent glance of Hitler and Mussolini. This France, they thought, would be anti-Liberal, anti-British, but (unlike Germany) not necessarily anticapitalist, or noncapitalist. It would be the France of *La France aux Français*. The grim and ugly paradox of the whole thing was that the slogan *La France aux Français* became the more or less official slogan of the French Government on the day when two-thirds of France's territory were under German occupation; and that this slogan, *La France aux Français,* was essentially one symbolizing the attempted fraternization of France with the Nazi conquerors! Equally grim is the thought that the "National Revolution" should have triumphed on the very day when France had departed from her true national tradition further than she had departed from it in a thousand years.

Jacques Maritain

THE FRENCH PEOPLE WAS NOT DECADENT

Jacques Maritain (1882–   ) came to the United States after the fall of France. He was Visiting Professor of Philosophy at Columbia and Princeton from 1940–1944, served as French Ambassador to the Holy See from 1945– 1948, and then returned to Princeton where he retired with the rank of Professor Emeritus in 1953. Maritain, who was converted to Catholicism in 1906, has gained fame as one of the leading contemporary exponents of neo-Thomism. The many commentaries, written in the immediate aftermath of defeat, which attributed France's plight to the moral collapse of her people, prompted Maritain to come to the defense of his compatriots.

From *France My Country: Through the Disaster,* by Jacques Maritain (Longmans, Green and Company, 1941), pp. 22–34. Used by permission of David McKay Company, Inc.

A people may live under a democracy that is breaking up without itself disintegrating in its inner personal life. The French people was vanquished; it was not decadent. It was not its taste for pleasure and a life of ease that led to the catastrophe, as certain official statements, broadcast at the very moment when an armistice was being solicited, cruelly insinuated. The failures for which the leaders are answerable—the leaders of all degrees and all the parties—the failures due to the bungling of the General Staff as well as of the statesmen, must not be laid at the door of those who when mobilization was decreed set forth with such admirable dignity, with such quiet, noble determination, who laid down their lives by the thousand.

I do not mean to say that in the deeper causes of the defeat the people did not have its share of responsibility. First and foremost of its faults is in having given itself such leaders. I am well aware that no nation can be entirely absolved of the leadership in which it has more or less acquiesced. I said further back that even before the war started, our people was politically demoralized. Its relation to its politicians was a highly peculiar one, though similar examples may be found elsewhere. It was what might be called in biological parlance a relationship of parasitical symbiosis. They put up with their parasites because they found certain specific advantages in playing host to them. They unloaded upon them their heavier responsibilities, they drew from them countless little private benefits, they used them as scapegoats to curse at when things went too badly; they took an interest and a vicarious part in their game after the fashion of amateur experts, ironically conniving with them, as it were, in their performances. For a long time they liked and mistrusted and endured them as they were, until the moment arrived— quite a few years back now—when they had just about enough of them.

It is well to point out, too, the sociological role played, in France as everywhere else, by the proletarization of the middle classes, the confusion and political instability to which it led and the chance it afforded to irresponsible mob leadership. And I might add another thing which seems to me extremely relevant. The French people, precisely, I daresay, because of its longer experience with political life and self-government, was in the thick of a wave of self-criticism at the very moment when, on the other side of the frontier, the totalitarian chieftains were laboring with all their might and means to rouse the masses to the highest pitch of unquestioned fanaticism. I recall an article I read early in the war by a young French university man—one of the finest representatives of the younger generation and a most ardent defender of liberty—which he had written to uphold the Allied cause in the foreign press. His paper was from beginning to end nothing but a soul-searching study in which all our shortcomings were subjected to merciless criticism. The gist of it all, I daresay, was: We are resolved to have done with all our mistakes. And I do think really that had the fates given French youth ten-years' leeway, it would have succeeded in bringing about an upswing in the country, spiritual as well as social and political, that would have astonished the world. However that may be, the fact remains that soul-searchings and self-depreciation are not the most favorable state of mind for making war.

But what I should like before all else to call attention to here is that the disaster-breeding weaknesses which characterized French political life and the causes of which I tried to point out further back—weaknesses, indeed, which might have been overcome by a great man, had God raised one up—were, like the political system of which they were an integral part, excrescences upon the surface of French public life, without root in the depths and realities of the national character. So long as a democracy is sound, its political life flows out of the rank and file of the mass of the people. When it begins to break up, politics becomes the trade of a clique of specialists and drifts ever farther away from the bedstream of the national life. Indeed our people continued to keep intact its qualities of civilized climate—of humane kindliness, of patient and diligent toil, of inborn mutual helpfulness. These virtues may lie unused, as happened in France for many years, through no fault but that of the politicians and their party oligarchies. They may for a time seem befuddled; they persist just the same.

After every catastrophe in history the minds of men are exposed to the temptation of taking refuge in a wholesale indictment of each and everyone's omissions and commissions, thus escaping the more difficult job of hunting down the real causes of misfortune. Laudable and stirring as it may be, this "escape into Ethics" contains also much self-delusion and weak-mindedness. In every human community, patently, evil plays a large part; it will always be easy, therefore, to find enough shortcomings in a beaten nation to indict it. It is ever easy, if not magnanimous, to pass harsh judgment upon the unfortunate.

There was much indecisiveness in France, much loose organization, negligence, slovenliness. Individualism run amuck. The standard of sexual morality, of civic and business ethics, was at a pretty low ebb, though it was unquestionably much higher than in the totalitarian states. In France at least people were still free to take stock of themselves, and the sense of individual responsibility was in private life more highly developed. The worst of it was the official treadmill, the bureaucratic machine which seemed purposely contrived to bar the way to posts of public authority for those who by their abilities were best fitted to fill them. All these blemishes doubtless contributed to the present catastrophe, but rather as remote factors than as basic and determining causes. That the defeat of France, like all great calamities, should bring with it an insistent demand from each and all for moral and spiritual regeneration is obvious. But it is utterly irrational to see in the sins of the French the direct and decisive reason for that defeat when the sins of their conquerors cry to heaven.

Whatever be the shortcomings that France may have to blame herself for, she has remained faithful to the values of the spirit, to the sense of what is human, true and free, to the quality of generous humility in every-day life. She knew how to accomplish much with little, she respected the dignity of those who chose to be poor so they might live by the dream within them, she was the sanctuary of art and poetry to the whole world. Her civilization, her wisdom, resided not in any thin top layer of aristocrats of the mind, but reached down to the very depths of the people. She was the spiritual home of the nations of the earth, the preeminently Christian land. Before this war French intellectual life was undergoing a brilliant revival. The boldest undertakings, the most noteworthy achievements were occurring in science, in industry, in the great technological plants. In the past twenty years or so a religious renaissance of the most genuine and fruitful kind was occurring in France, both in the spiritual field and in that of social service, and its harvest was now being brought in among the working-class youth. The French Catholics had assimilated religious persecution, profiting by it to achieve their independence of the state, to revive in themselves the sense of the Gospel, to live and feel with the people, to kindle, with a spirit and dash meet for any conquest, a most active apostolic flame. The French people was *politically* demoralized; it was not *morally* demoralized.

I remember the months of August and September 1939. Faced with events dreadful beyond all bounds, the French people maintained—to its honor, be it said, as well as in explanation of its weakness—a sense of balance, of human truthfulness, of plain duty freely submitted to; and its manner of expressing this, without ringing phrases, without flag-waving, was one of the most beautiful and heart-rending things to be seen on this earth. "Mr. Hitler is not a gentleman," was how the barber put it in the little town where I happened to be a few days before mobilization. This understatement meant that if Mr. Hitler did not stop, the barber and his friends were, for their part, inclined to do what was needful to render the relations between nations "more gentlemanly." The French people had no hatred for the Germans; Nazism seemed to them a disgraceful lot of foolishness, the war a stupid business. But their political instinct was keener than that of their leaders, and this instinct had made them sense for some time past that what was happening on the other side of the Rhine, combined with the backbonelessness of those who for the moment held the reins at home, would some day make that stupid calamity inevitable. That day having arrived, they had not a moment's hesitation as to what they must do. Except for the Communists, the people with one accord accepted the war as a nasty chore which there was no shirking. They went into it with grave faces and a heavy heart, hoping that it would not turn them aside from their real work too long, their minds made up that when it was over everything would have to be overhauled, and in the meantime determined to wage a genuine war. They could not understand why the Germans were not attacked right off, while they were busy in Poland, still less why the Allies did not push Italy to the wall; it was all the more incomprehensible as at that time everyone believed that, aviation apart, the arsenals of France were short of nothing. A war that was not a war looked suspicious to them; and General Gamelin's system came to them as the first disillusionment, the first premonitory heartache, to which, however, they resigned themselves hopefully. (Later on they were to fall into step only too blithely with the psychology of that system.) They submitted with infinite patience—though beneath that patience much disgust was gradually going to collect—to the way the censored press and the radio treated them like infants and kept on ladling out drivel.

There was precious little ideology in their makeup. For them the things at issue were quite simple, quite concrete, quite elementary things, and they did not see how there could be any compromise upon them. It was a question of the right to breathe freely, of getting up of a morning without being eyed by a police officer, of going ungovernessed to a freely chosen job, instead of being forcibly coralled into a labor camp, of the right to criticize the government and to read the papers which, while little stock could be taken in them, at least did not lie in chorus at the behest of the state. It was a question of the right to get married without having first to stop at the veterinary's, or to wonder whether one had not a grandmother somewhere with a would-be taint in her blood; of being free to bring up children according to one's own ideas and to say before them all that one thought, and even a bit more, without having to fear their turning informer to the police against their parents. It had to do with planning one's life unhampered, which, though it had indeed become bitter and care-ridden these last six or seven years, was still a life of men, not of cattle; and with preserving untarnished the heritage of patience, intelligence, and freedom handed down by fathers and grandfathers, and preparing all the while for the day when mankind should live a life more just and humane.

This is why the average Frenchman understood that the time had come to say "No" once and for all to the Nazi will to aggression. . . . It meant that the war which he went into was a war for civilization—that it was no mere national quarrel, no mere gang-busting expedition, that it was neither a holy war nor a struggle over ideologies, but a battle for civilization.

What a pity that this straight thinking and sound instinctive feeling could not be crystallized into a clear and solid political consciousness!

If the world could have seen how such men set forth, and then what was done to them by incompetents, pessimistic patriots and receivers in bankruptcy, it would have cause to remember what Charles Péguy said concerning "la politique" befouling "la mystique." But it is not of "la mystique" that we are speaking here; it is only of sheer healthy instinct. If the French rulers of our day remind us of the advisers of Charles VII, the people they governed did not have the conquering faith of Jeanne d'Arc; they were just good, brave and sensible Frenchmen.

V CONCLUSIONS

Edouard Bonnefous

POLITICAL AND MILITARY RESPONSIBILITIES FOR THE DEFEAT OF 1940

The busy career of Edouard Bonnefous (1907–   ) has been marked by success in both the political and academic worlds. He represented the department of Seine-et-Oise in the National Assembly from 1946 to 1958, and held a variety of portfolios in a number of ministries during the Fourth Republic. He moved on to the Senate in 1959 and was re-elected by the same constituency in October 1968. He concurrently holds the rank of Professor at the Institut des Hautes Etudes Internationales. *Upon his father's death in 1956, Edouard Bonnefous took on the task of completing the former's projected seven-tome* Histoire Politique de la Troisième République, *of which two volumes had been published at the time. The following summary of his concluding remarks appeared in the* Revue Politique et Parlementaire *prior to the completion of this important contribution to the historiography of modern France.*

"The Third Republic died of its errors. The mistakes committed by the succeeding governments inevitably led to military defeat and the regime's downfall." This accusation, first levelled by Pierre Laval and often echoed by a number of others, finally convinced both the partisans of the Vichy Regime and their political opponents. Abolished by the followers of Marshal Pétain, the Third Republic was not restored by De Gaulle in 1944.

Is it true that the political personnel and governments of the Third Republic were *solely* responsible for the military and political events of 1939–1940? Certainly not. Conveniently forgetting that in 1940 a number of military leaders were more concerned with the salvation of the Army than that of the State, the enemies of the parliamentary system, for nearly thirty years, have performed a tour de force by lending broad credence to the fiction that the war was lost by the politicians. The Vichy Government argued its case against the regime before the Court at Riom. But the proceedings came to an abrupt halt as soon as it realized that the Army itself was on trial.

From Edouard Bonnefous, "Les Responsabilités politiques et militaires de la défaite de 1940," *Revue Politique et Parlementaire,* LXIX (May 1967), pp. 27–38. Reprinted by permission of the *Revue Politique et Parlementaire.* [Editor's translation.]

This Manichean verdict is unacceptable. It is much too exclusive and categorical an interpretation of history. One might as well proclaim that France owed her victory in 1918 to the Third Republic alone. This would leave out the involvement of the Allies, the intervention of the United States, and the splendid contributions of Joffre, Foch, Weygand and Pétain—to mention only the role played by the military leaders. Both in peacetime and wartime, the responsibilities of political leaders are linked to those of military leaders to the extent that the former support the latter and give them free rein. The civilian authority is always supreme. The strongest criticism which one can direct against the statesmen of the period is that they placed too much faith in a High Command which was incapable of adapting itself to modern times. Whether it was a question of the efficient use of credits voted by Parliament, or the intensive rearmament of Germany, of which one and all were well aware, it seems that the Executive Power was unable to act in a manner which would assure the security of the land. On the one hand, the succeeding governments were not strong enough to make major decisions against the advice of respected and powerful military experts, whose glorious reputations had been won on the battlefields of the Great War. On the other hand, the constant turnover of ministries made impossible the formulation and enacting of bolder policies.

The normal functioning of our political institutions was hampered by the deterioration of parliamentary ethics. Even more harmful was the dearth of first-rate statesmen. The Republic had been served with distinction in the past, from Gambetta and Waldeck-Rousseau to Clemenceau and Poincaré. After 1930 the quality of the political personnel was below par. During the years 1932–1940, that is to say after Hitler's rise to power, France underwent a series of serious crises for which the Right and the Left are equally responsible. The riots of February 1934 and the haphazard reforms following the elections of 1936 shook and divided the nation, even while, on the other side of the Rhine, the utmost energy was being devoted to the single-minded purpose of preparing a war of revenge. In the face of the sustained policies which Hitler and Mussolini were then enforcing in their respective countries, France could ill afford to be governed by twenty ministries in eight years.

The need to repair the material destruction of the Great War and domestic and international financial problems had imposed a very heavy burden on the French economy. Morally, the nation was not ready, on the morrow of a long and hard conflict, to sacrifice its hopes for a higher standard of living in order to prepare for a new war which many did not believe to be in the offing. The French long held to the illusion that the Great War would be "the war to end wars." Did not the most respected statesmen proclaim their faith in the League of Nations, disarmament and collective security? For a while the French sought to forget and to enjoy life. The heady years of the immediate postwar period came to an end with the crisis of 1930.

Henceforth economizing and the reduction of the national budget were the order of the day. If Frenchmen were resigned, albeit without enthusiasm, to accept a seemingly inevitable tightening of the belt, they were not yet ready to make moral and material sacrifices in order to prepare for war against Hitler and Nazism. The low ebb of the French military establishment was reached in 1936. In the name of economy, the French officer corps was to be reduced from 30 thousand to 25 thousand. By the time this policy was rescinded, 1,800 posts had been abolished. The shortening of the length of the period of compulsory military service was a perennial goal of the Left. In 1936, the number of men to be called to the colors was set at under 200 thousand. During this period, only the Extreme Right clamored for the strengthening of the Army. As we shall see, it was prompted both by a genuine concern for national defense and ulterior political motives. Can we then conclude, as the Vichy Government charged at the Riom trials, that the defeat of 1940 was due to the industrial and military policies of the Popular Front?

Even after 1936, the Left continued to be pacifist. True, it was ready to intervene in Spain and denounced Hitler and Mussolini. But this was a very slow evolution. The Leftist members of Parliament traditionally voted against military appropriations. After 1919, the Left consistently championed pacifism and disarmament. It went so far as to argue that a firm foreign policy represented a threat to peace. Munich brought about a radical change in the attitude of the Left, which then began to advocate military intervention to bring Hitler to heel. This new stand was doubtless a reflection of the Soviet Union's opposition to the policies of Chamberlain and Daladier. Unfortunately, the Left failed to ponder our country's actual chances in an eventual conflict.

It cannot be denied that the great strikes of 1936, and sporadic work stoppages in 1937 and 1938, seriously disrupted the armament industries. Production was so deficient that it was impossible to step up the pace to a satisfactory level once war had been declared. During the first six months of the conflict only 360 thousand shells were produced. During the same period in 1914–1915, our factories had turned out 1 million. Still, one must recognize that when it came to appropriations, Léon Blum did much better than his predecessors. His successors did equally well right down to the outbreak of the war.

All in all, however, the pace of the armaments program was much too slow during the immediate prewar period. When Paul Reynaud became Minister of Finance, November 1, 1938, he came to the conclusion that national security depended upon stepped-up production. "Do you really believe that in today's Europe, France can maintain her standard of living, spend twenty-five billions for armaments and rest two days a week?" he asked in a radio broadcast. But the Daladier-Reynaud program gained no more support from the Left than it did from the Right. At the Congress of the C.G.T., February 16, 1938, Jouhaux warned: "If those in power refuse to heed the working class, it will know how to defend its interests." The C.G.T. then called for a general strike. Paul Reynaud continued to urge the workers and the unions to help increase production. On the day Czechoslovakia was erased from the map, April 25, 1939, he reminded his countrymen in another broadcast: "A France of forty million people living next to a nation of eighty million inhabitants who labor sixty hours a week must work harder than any other country in the world." The next day in *Le Populaire,* Léon Blum expressed indignation at this unwarranted evocation of the foreign peril for domestic political purposes. Earlier, in September 1938, 'at the time of the Sudeten crisis, Jules Moch had asked: Work harder. Why?"

After 1938, a dual trend becomes discernible on the Right. Some Rightists, animated by their hostility toward the Popular Front and by fear of Communism, came to the conclusion that a change of regime was imperative. Others, attracted by Fascism and convinced of the need for a *rapprochement* with Germany, felt that France should sever its traditional ties and work for a Franco-German alignment. In conservative circles, the revolutionary threat loomed larger than the dangers presented by the new German regime. The first line of defense was at home. These political pretexts led to the abandonment of an old national tradition. The bourgeoisie then came to believe that an understanding with Fascist Italy was imperative, and that a *modus vivendi* with Germany was not only possible but desirable. These ideas were first spread by a few intellectuals, who lumped them with their attacks on the Bourgeois State, the capitalist system and parliamentarism. They began to gather momentum when the economic crisis hit the lower bourgeoisie. The opposition to the regime and the parliamentarians was most outspoken in those social classes which made up the rank and file of the War Veterans' organizations. As French Conservatives saw it, standing up to Nazi Germany was not a national priority—especially after the advent of the Popular Front.

All the while, the Army was plotting. The lessons of the Franco epic, where the military succeeded in overthrowing the Republic and restoring order, were not lost. General de Castelnau, the spokesman for the military bourgeoisie, kept the Right in a constant state of alarm in 1936, by drawing parallels between the French and Spanish situations in his articles in *L'Echo de Paris*. According to him, the "bolshevik revolution" was at our door and the parliamentary regime was defenseless. It was up to the Army to take over. Although large numbers of republican officers shied from the prospects of a civil war, many were those who were willing to carry out a coup d'état. A number of very active clandestine networks were formed at the time. Men like Loustanau-Lacau, Pétain's assistant, and Colonel Groussard, Franchet d'Esperey's chief of staff, played a major role in the infiltration of the Army, and what can only be called its "demoralization." The political doctrines of Vichy were to stem from the anti-Communist networks of the Army.

The politicians of the interwar period have often been accused of having been blind to the trends of the time, and of having failed to perceive the means to salvation. In their defense, it may be argued that they were operating in a polluted atmosphere of intrigues and scandals, compounded by virulent press campaigns. After 1930, the French political scene was disrupted by the pressure of Rightist movements (Action française, Leagues, clandestine organizations, etc.). They may never have enjoyed broad popular support, but they were violent, well organized and widespread. The country seemed to be on the edge of revolution, and many yearned for the "law and order" which then prevailed in Germany and Italy. Future generations will find it difficult to sense, through their history books, the climate of violence which for nearly a decade crippled the institutions of the Third Republic, at the very time when both Parliament and the Government were in dire need of the broadest possible base of support.

The revolutionary Extreme Left must bear its share of the blame for the climate of insecurity which then permeated the country. The parades, with their Red flags and raised clenched fists, the sit-down strikes, and the bloody brawls frightened the moderates. The Extreme Left was all the more intransigent because it was not really representative of the working class and felt the need to gain recognition as a new political force. Did all this revolutionary agitation present an actual threat to existing institutions? Today, one wonders. What matters is that segments of the bourgeoisie felt threatened at the time and began to believe that a change of regime was the only way out. From then on the Third Republic was shaken from within by what had traditionally been essentially conservative circles.

Every morning, or every week, the press of the Extreme Right (*Gringoire, Je suis partout, Le Matin, L'Action française,* etc.) dispensed insults and calumnies, and blackmailed those politicians who had dared to ignore the advice and directives issued by the leaders of the extremist movements. It is impossible to understand this period, or to account for the behavior of the parliamentarians and the ministers, unless one keeps in mind the impact of these relentless attacks by men who had become blinded by their passions. Nationalists ready to collaborate with the enemy and apostles of order ready to launch a civil war, together worked to paralyze and undermine the regime at a crucial hour when the interests of France called for national unity. In those same circles where the defense of order had been an age-old tradition, a large majority were now tearing at the very foundations of the State.

In the realm of the military a number of grievous errors were committed. First, in the immediate aftermath of the war, instead of thinking ahead to the wars of the future, we formulated our military doctrines on the basis of the type of fighting that had just come to an end. Second, we opted for a defensive strategy although our foreign policy implied the intervention of offensive units beyond our borders. Third, having committed ourselves to a defensive strategy, we failed to fortify the Northern border—the traditional path of invasion. Fourth, even though the Government and the High Command were fully aware of the extent of German rearmament and of the emphasis placed on mechanization, we failed to adapt our war material and organization to those of the enemy. Let us now probe these questions a little more thoroughly.

As soon as the First World War came to an end, our military leaders were confronted with the task of formulating new concepts of national defense in the light of the experience of the recent conflict, and in keeping with the aims of French foreign policy. Unfortunately, the High Command wavered too long before coming to a decision, and it was never unanimous when making recommendations to the Government. On their part, the succeeding ministries were never able to impose strategic policies of their own, and they placed too much confidence in military leaders who proved incapable of harmonizing our military plans with our diplomatic options.

The need for heavy fortifications along our northern and eastern borders was obvious. Marshal Joffre, who was still acting as an advisor in 1919, proposed the creation of a succession of fortified regions spread around the main strategic strongholds from Belfort to Dunkirk. But he had to bow before the opposition of Marshal Pétain. It was certainly a mistake to appoint Marshal Pétain to positions of influence during the interwar period. He himself underlined the magnitude of the mistake, when, on July 10, 1947, he told a Parliamentary Investigating Commission: "After the War of 1914–1918, it was all over. In military matters, mine was a closed mind. When I realized that other tools, weapons and methods were being used, I must admit that I lost interest." Yet, as early as 1920, this "closed" mind became Vice-President of the Supreme War Council and Technical Advisor to the Ministry of War. He assumed the added responsibilities of Inspector-General of the Army in 1922, and of Chief-of-Staff of National Defense in 1931. Minister of War from

February to November 1934, Minister of State for a few days in June 1935, he always remained an influential member of the Supreme Council of National Defense. In 1939, he was given the sensitive post of Ambassador to Madrid.

Pétain was a fervent advocate of the doctrine of the continuous front, with a network of trenches as in 1917. His strong opposition to offensive theory and practice had earned him the reputation of being a defeatist, most unjustly let it be said, before he became the "Victor of Verdun." But failing to push his doctrines to their logical conclusion, he deemed that it was not necessary to fortify the Belgian border or the line of the Ardennes. In 1932, Marshal Pétain caused the Supreme War Council to turn down an appropriation of 240 million francs proposed by the Minister of War, François Piétri, to fortify Maubeuge, Montmédy, and Valenciennes. Generals Weygand and Gamelin voted in favor of the Minister's proposal.

While Pétain was Minister of War in the Cabinet of Gaston Doumergue, he stubbornly put his pet theories into practice. A month after he took office, he testified before the Senate Army Committee. Some of its members had expressed concern because the traditional invasion route remained unprotected. Declared Pétain: "The Ardennes forests begin at Montmédy. The setting up of special defense works can make them impenetrable. Consequently we consider this to be a zone of destruction. Naturally, the edges of the forest closest to the enemy would be protected. There, we would erect some pillboxes. But the enemy would not advance on this front because it is too shallow. Should he do so, we would nip him at the other end. Thus this is not a dangerous sector" *(sic)*. This reputedly "safe" sector was the one where Corap's Army was mauled and routed even before it could find the spot where it might "nip" the enemy. The Maginot Line, built from 1929 to 1936, was a reflection of this line of thinking. At the moment of truth, Hitler would simply bypass it. In the meantime, it gave France a false sense of security and led the Army to concentrate on the formation of garrison units, which were not even given a chance, in 1940, to put to use the only type of military training they had ever received.

Our purely defensive strategy was in flagrant contradiction to our diplomacy and alliances. Our foreign policy dictated radically different military planning. Since there were fewer than 40 million

Frenchmen as against 65 million Germans, we could only make up this numerical deficiency through the support of our Little Entente allies. Together, we added up to 125 million people—approximately the size of the population of the United States at the time. The effectiveness of this threat against Germany from the East depended, however, on our unequivocal enforcement of the principle of collective security. In other words, we had to envisage the intervention of French military forces whenever Germany threatened the *status quo*. At Locarno, France implicitly recognized that the question of Germany's eastern borders was not definitely settled. Yet we decided to restrict ourselves to the sole defense of our own frontiers. This ostrich-like policy was conducive to national security only to the extent that our defensive network was impregnable. This did not prove to be the case. Again, in view of the determining role he played in the formulation of our strategy during the interwar period, Marshal Pétain must bear a large share of the blame because he failed to push his concepts to their logical conclusion. While committed to the doctrine of the continuous front, he did not deem it necessary to fortify either the region behind the Ardennes forest or the Belgian frontier. Our foreign policy should have prompted our military leaders to make provisions for offensive maneuvers. They failed to do so.

Our best-equipped, crack units were destroyed in Belgium. How in the world could we commit such a blunder? The advance into Belgium was both illogical and contrary to our basic defensive strategic concepts. The fact that the attack would come from the North was obvious. It was further confirmed by all the information at hand. On this point, the testimonies of military and political witnesses are equally devastating. Our military intelligence services and our diplomats were well aware of the German plan of attack. Our High Command knew the date set for the German offensive many days in advance. It had even been confirmed by the Vatican through unofficial channels. The Dutch, who had also been warned, acted accordingly. General Gamelin did not budge. This failure to act, which accounts for the swift success of the German onslaught and is the primary cause of the debacle, remains unexplainable by the historian. One must never try to rewrite history. But one cannot refrain from speculating as to what might have happened if Gamelin had immediately recalled all the men of leave; if he had concentrated our effectives at strategic points; if he had restricted all means of transportation to military uses; and if, on J-Day, he had not delayed the launching of the "Belgium-Luxembourg" maneuver (a counterpart of the Dyle maneuver). In 1947, testifying before the Parliamentary Investigating Commission, General Gamelin explained his failure to take immediate action on the grounds that he "did not want to multiply the number of false alarms," and that he "wanted to make sure that the enemy was really on the offensive."

The French offensive in Belgium was thus doomed from the start. It was suicidal to order troops trained exclusively for defensive operations to abandon some of our most vulnerable positions, and to send them into a territory that had been poorly reconnoitered. Moreover, since there were differences in the rate of mobility of the various units, they took up their new position in staggered order. Even before contact had been made with the enemy, we had managed to dislocate our forces along the most exposed frontier.

The High Command had remained deaf to all warnings. On March 9, 1940, a report by Messieurs Frammont and Taittinger, who had inspected the Montmédy-Sedan front on behalf of the Army Committee of the Chamber of Deputies, pointed out, to no avail, the rudimentary, quasi-embryonic condition of the defense installations. Equally unheeded went the entreaties of M. Félix Grat, a deputy and a captain in a commando unit, who urged, at a secret meeting of the Committee on April 19, the strengthening of the defensive network along the border between France and Luxembourg. After seven months of inaction, the planned entrenchments had yet to be completed. The destruction and ravages attributable to the *Panzers* and *Stukas* attest to the fact that the uncoordinated use of tanks and planes, weapons in which our High Command did not really believe, was another great mistake. The *Stukas* were especially effective because our anti-aircraft equipment was well nigh nonexistent.

Like all the influential members of the High Command, Pétain made no bones about his lack of faith in the armored divisions advocated by General Estienne. As early as 1933, in articles published in the *Revue politique et parlementaire,* and in a book, *L'Armée de Métier,* which appeared a year later, Lieutenant Colonel De Gaulle had explained the full potential of this type of weapon. Our High Command was fully aware of the use which the German Army was making of this French idea. On November 20, 1935, General Renondeau, military attaché at the French Embassy in Berlin, had sent his superiors a detailed report on the organization of the new German armored units. His report read in part: "The most striking thing is the small ratio of infantry and artillery in proportion to the number of tanks." Nevertheless, the Supreme War Council consistently opposed the formation of armored units—although Gamelin seems to have gradually become reconciled to the idea after 1936. Even while Hitler was launching the German rearmament program, Pétain agreed to a reduction by one-third of the credits allocated to experimentation with new weapons.

Provisions were made for our tanks to remain to the rear and to act in support of the infantry. Some attack tanks were designed to precede the infantry against limited objectives. The latter carried only enough fuel for five hours of continuous operation. This shortsighted policy continued to prevail in 1939, after the Polish campaign, in spite of a most instructive report sent to the Government by our military attaché in Warsaw. He concluded: "There is every likelihood that the methods in the Polish campaign will be applied again in certain sectors of the Western front. Now that we are familiar with them, we are in excellent position to devise effective counter-measures." In October 1939, Colonel de Gaulle, whose theories had just been validated, sent a note to General Headquarters in which he sought to explain that our use of tanks in scattered units provided no effective defense against the massive thrusts of the enemy. General Georges deemed that his suggestions were "interesting," and that they were worthy of "further study." Nothing had been done by May 1940, when the enemy gave a demonstration which settled the argument once and for all.

If the French Army was not as powerful, in 1939, as it could or should have been, it would nevertheless be incorrect to argue that our country did not then possess the necessary weapons. The real explanations for our weakened condition must be sought elsewhere.

Marc Bloch

A FRENCHMAN EXAMINES
HIS CONSCIENCE

*In few men have professional and personal integrity been so happily blended
as in Marc Bloch (1886–1944). Not only has the quality of his work earned
him a permanent place among the foremost French medievalists, but he
invariably won the respect and devotion of those with whom he came into
contact. Bloch, who served as a lieutenant in both world wars, joined a
Resistance group after he was demobilized, and was captured and executed
by the Germans in 1944. His remains were not found and identified until after
the Liberation. Written in 1940 and first published in 1946, L'Etrange Défaite
was in a sense Bloch's testament as a historian. From all standpoints, it is
difficult to think of anyone better fitted to inquire into the reasons for France's
collapse.*

We have just suffered such a defeat as no one would have believed
possible. On whom or on what should the blame be laid? On the
French system of parliamentary government, say our generals; on
the rank and file of the fighting services, on the English, on the fifth
column—in short, on any and everybody except themselves. Old
Joffre was wiser. "Whether I was responsible for the winning of the
Battle of the Marne," he said, "I do not know. But of this I feel pretty
certain, that, had it been lost, the failure would have been laid at my
door." He intended, by that remark, to remind us that a commanding
officer is responsible for everything that happens while he is in
supreme charge of events. Whether the initiative for each separate
decision comes directly from him, whether in each instance he knows
what is being done, is beside the point. The mere fact that he has
accepted the position of "Chief" means that he must take upon his
shoulders the burden of failure as well as the panoply of success.
The great truth which that simple man expressed so unequivocally is
seen today to have an even deeper meaning. When the Army was
disbanded after the final campaign, it would have been hard to find
a single officer among those with whom I was in daily contact who

From Marc Bloch, *Strange Defeat: A Statement of Evidence Written in 1940*, translated by Gerard Hopkins (London: Oxford University Press, 1949), pp. 25, 36, 126–127,
130–132, 132–140, 143, 156, 157–159, 160, 161–166, 167–171, 175–176. Reprinted by
permission of Librairie Armand Colin, Paris.

had the slightest doubt on the subject. Whatever the deep-seated causes of the disaster may have been, the immediate occasion was the utter incompetence of the High Command. . . . What drove our armies to disaster was the cumulative effect of a great number of different mistakes. One glaring characteristic is, however, common to all of them. Our leaders, or those who acted for them, were incapable of thinking in terms of a *new* war. In other words, the German triumph was, essentially, a triumph of intellect—and it is that which makes it so peculiarly serious. . . .

In no nation is any professional group ever entirely responsible for its own actions. The solidarity of society as a whole is too strong to permit the existence of the sort of moral autonomy, existing in isolation, which any such responsibility would seem to imply. The staffs worked with tools which were put into their hands by the nation at large. The psychological conditions in which they lived were not altogether of their own making, and they themselves, through their members, were as their origins had molded them. They could be only what the totality of the social *fact,* as it existed in France, permitted them to be. That is why I cannot rest content with what I have so far written. I trust that I am honest; certainly, I have done my best to describe, in the terms of my own experience, what I believe to have been the vices of our military system, and the part played by them in the defeat of my country. But, unless I am to be guilty of betraying a trust, I must go farther. The very nature of my inquiry makes it necessary that the evidence of the soldier be balanced and completed by the self-examination of the Frenchman.

I do not joyfully or lightly embark on this part of my task. As a Frenchman I feel constrained, in speaking of my country, to say of her only what is good. It is a harsh duty that compels a man to make a public show of his mother's weaknesses when she is in misery and despair. As an historian, I know better than do most men how difficult it is to conduct an analysis which, if it is to have any value, must be concerned with a complex of causes, remote, involved, and, in the present state of sociological science, extremely difficult to uncover. But personal scruples are, in this matter, wholly unimportant. My children, when they read this balance-sheet of history, the unknown friends into whose hands it may someday come, must not be allowed to reproach its author with having played tricks with truth, of having condemned a number of glaring faults, while, at the same time, maintaining a deliberate silence about errors for which every citizen was, in part, responsible.

The men at the front are rarely satisfied with their companions in the rear. It needs an unusually large dose of generosity, when one is sleeping on the hard ground, to forgive old friends the comfort of their beds, or, when machine-guns are rat-tatting over one's head, to think without bitterness of the prosperous security of shops still crammed with customers and the peaceful delights of provincial cafés to the habitués of which war means no more than leisurely discussions of points of strategical theory. It is when battle ends in disaster that the gulf separating these two halves of the nation threatens to become permanent. The soldier is only too conscious of the sacrifices he has been called upon to make. If they turn out to have been useless, that, he feels, is not *his* responsibility. His leaders, ever fearful of his criticism, encourage him to find scapegoats anywhere rather than in the Army. Thus is born the fatal legend of the "stab in the back" which reactionary movements and military *coups d'état* always find so useful. I hope that in what I have so far written I have made it clear that some, at least, of the veterans of 1940 will refuse to listen to such sowers of discord. But it is no use pretending that the back areas were not, to some extent, as deserving of blame as the armies. . . .

Confronted by the nation's peril and by the duties that it lays on every citizen, all adults are equal, and only a curiously warped mind would claim for any of them the privilege of immunity. What, after all, *is* a "civilian" in time of war? He is nothing more than a man whose weight of years, whose health, whose profession (if it be judged essential to the well-being of his country) prevents him from bearing arms effectively. To find himself thus kept from serving his fellows in the one way that any citizen would wish to do is a misfortune for any man. Why should it confer on him the right to escape the common danger? In a few years from now I shall be too old for mobilization. My sons will take my place. Am I, therefore, to conclude that my life has become more precious than theirs? Far better, on the contrary, that their youth should be preserved, if necessary, at the cost of my gray hairs. Herodotus said, a long time ago, that the great impiety of war is that it forces fathers to consign their children to the tomb. Should it be a matter of complaint for us that Nature's law has once more come into its own? For the nation at large there can be no worse tragedy than having to sacrifice those very lives on which her destiny reposes. Against the strength of those young bodies we others weigh but lightly in the scale. Nor do I except the women, save only those young mothers whose survival is necessary in the interests of their children. Girls today laugh at the swooning habits of their grandmothers. They are right to do so, and I am certain that courage in them is no less natural than in us, nor less a duty. In the days of professional armies the soldier, whether knight or mercenary, shed his blood for his patron, and for this service the noncombatants paid in rents and wages. If he put their safety in peril they had a just ground of complaint, for the contract had been broken. Today, when every fit man is a soldier, no one in the menaced city can escape the tedium and the risks. To share them is his bounden duty. To maintain otherwise is mere sentimentality—or cowardice.

These self-evident truths are so simple that one feels a certain shame at having to call men's attention to them. But were they generally understood in the course of those months through which we lived but recently? I find it hard to believe. Too many mayors thought it their duty to ask that their towns should not be defended; too many leaders, military as well as civilian, were only too willing to act in accordance with this fallacious conception of the public interest. Truth to tell, such timid souls were not moved solely by the wish—in itself admirable—to save human lives. The fearful destruction of property that had accompanied the war of 1914–1918 left bitter memories. Everybody knew that the artistic heritage of the country had been cruelly mutilated, and our national prosperity to a large extent compromised. There was a feeling that it would be better to accept any humiliation rather than undergo a second time this twin impoverishment. It was a strange form of wisdom that did not even ask whether, in fact, there could be any worse catastrophe, for our culture or for the system of our economic life, than to let ourselves be conquered by a robber society.

A day came when the decision was taken to declare all cities of more than 20,000 inhabitants "open." That a village lived in by poor yokels should be bombed, smashed, and burned was, apparently, a matter of indifference to the noble apostles of humanity who upheld this view. But a city of solid tradesmen was quite another matter! . . . And so it came about that while the cadets of Saumur were being killed on the Loire, the enemy had already cut the bridges behind them at Nantes, because these were regarded as being "out of bounds." It is no good mincing words. This timidity of the nation at large was, no doubt, in many cases but the sum of the timidity of individuals. There were cases of officials leaving their posts without orders. Many instructions to evacuate were issued before they need have been. A sort of frenzy of flight swept over the whole country. It was no rare thing, along the roads crowded with refugees, to come on complete local fire-brigades perched on their engines. At the first rumor of the enemy's advance, off they had rushed to find safety for their persons and their property. I am convinced that they had been *told* to do so. Their towns could perish in the flames, provided the means of mastering the blaze could be got out of the danger-zone. . . . Such, it will be said, are ever the ways of bureaucracy. Alas! the evil went a great deal deeper than that. I know of at least one industrial center where, on the approach of the German columns, the managers hastily abandoned the factories without even bothering to see that their workpeople were paid. Had they been called up for service in one of the armed services, they would probably have stuck gamely to their posts. But they were "civilians," and, as such, they forgot, or had not been sufficiently reminded, that in time of war private professional interests no longer exist. When the nation is in arms, only one thing matters—the fighting front. . . .

Whatever the reasons, there can be no doubt that our governors, both individually and as a class, did lack something of that ruthless heroism which becomes so necessary when the country is in danger. But this very question of "governing class" raises questions which need very careful consideration. In the France of 1939 the members of the upper middle class were never sick of declaring that they had lost all power. This was an exaggeration. Solidly supported by the banks and the Press, the régime of the *élite* was not, to that extent, "finished." But it *is* true that the great industrialists no longer held a monopoly in the running of the country. The leaders of the principal trade unions, and, to a smaller extent, the mass of the wage-earners, had risen to a position of power in the affairs of the Republic. That had been obvious in 1938, when a certain minister—a "Man of Munich" if ever there was one—used them as intermediaries when he set about spreading an atmosphere of panic in order to cover up his own weakness. There can be no denying that if much heavy responsibility rested on the shoulders of the military authorities, a considerable amount of blame must also be laid at the door of the trade unions.

I am about to speak of matters of which I have no first-hand knowledge. I need hardly stress the fact that the life of the factory, both before and during the period of hostilities, lay far outside my normal field of operations. But the evidence which I have amassed is so unanimous, and comes from so many different sources, ranging in variety from chief engineers to machine-minders, that I am forced to accept its conclusions as valid. The output of our war factories was insufficient. We were not turning out enough airplanes, engines, or tanks. I do not for a moment believe that it was only, or even principally, the wage-earners who were to blame for this state of affairs. On the other hand, it would ill become them to plead complete innocence. Forgetful of the fact that they too, in their own way, were just as much soldiers as the men in uniform, they thought first and foremost about selling their labor at the highest price: in other words, about doing as little as possible, for the shortest time possible, in return for as much money as possible. In normal times that would be a perfectly natural attitude. "Sordid materialism!" once exclaimed a certain politician whose own enthusiasm for the spiritual was not, I should have said, particularly obvious. But that, of course, is sheer nonsense. The manual worker is out to sell the strength of his arms. The men who sell textiles, sugar, or armaments are scarcely in a position to be shocked if he applies to his own case the great law of trade, which is to give little and to receive much. But however legitimate that point of view may be at other times, it is cruelly out of place when the very existence of one's country is at stake, and when those at the front are risking their lives. The plumber of the village where I live told me that when he was called up to work in a war factory the other men used to hide his tools to prevent him from turning out more, or working more quickly, than was permitted by the unwritten "law" of the shop. That is an undeniable fact, and it provides a terrible indictment. But to suppose for a moment that that kind of indifference to the interests of the nation was general in one whole class of the population would be the height of injustice. I am more than ready to admit that there were honorable exceptions. Still, this attitude was quite widely enough spread for its consequences to weigh heavily in the scales of war. How it arose at all needs to be explained.

It has been said again and again, and by all sorts of people, that this war failed to rouse the deepest feelings of the nation to a much larger extent than did the last one. I believe that view to be entirely wrong. Our people are temperamentally disinclined actively to *want* any war. No Frenchman in 1939 burned with the desire to "die for Danzig." But then it is equally true to say that in 1914 none of them was particularly anxious to "die for Belgrade." The *camarilla* which hatched its plots around the Serbian throne was no more familiar to our workers and peasants than was, twenty years later, the corrupt government of Polish colonels; nor if it had been would it have fanned them to a white heat of enthusiasm. As to Alsace-Lorraine, though it is, no doubt, true that when the actual fighting began in 1914, a picture of the martyred provinces did suddenly emerge in men's minds from that decent obscurity which, only a few days earlier, had still shrouded it, but that was merely under the pressure of a necessity which, for quite other reasons, had already been accepted by the nation. Since we had been forced to take up arms, it was difficult to imagine that we should lay them down before we had delivered our lost brothers. Certainly, the beautiful Alsatian eyes, which the popular prints of the time were so fond of depicting, would never, of themselves, have had sufficient influence, in peacetime, on a public opinion which was concerned only to maintain the security of the nation's homes; would never have persuaded men lightly to launch their country on an adventure bristling with the most appalling dangers, with the sole object of drying those bewitching tears.

The truth of the matter is that on both occasions the national response drew its vigor from the same source. *"They're* always picking a quarrel with the rest of the world. The more we give 'em, the more they'll want. It just can't go on like this."* That was what one of my neighbors in a little village of the Creuse said to me shortly before I left for Strasbourg. A peasant of 1914 would have expressed himself in much the same words. As a matter of fact, if either of the two wars was more likely than the other to appeal to the deepest instincts of the masses, and especially of the industrial masses, it was undoubtedly the second, and that was because of the very "ideological" complexion which so many have blamed, but which did succeed in giving a touch of beauty to the sacrifices entailed. The men of the factories and the fields would no more, in 1939, have *deliberately* shed their blood for the overthrow of the dictators than would their elders of 1914 for the liberation of Alsace-Lorraine. But once the battle had been joined against those same dictators, and as a result of *their* action, they felt that by fighting they were helping forward one of the great tasks of humanity. To believe otherwise is to show complete ignorance of the high nobility which lies unexpressed in the hearts of a people which, like ours, has behind it a long history of political action. The absurd ineptitude of our official propaganda, its irritating and crude optimism, its timidity, and, above all, the inability of our rulers to give a frank definition of their war aims, may well, during the long months of inaction, have muddied to some extent what, in the early days, had been so crystal-clear. In May 1940 the spirit that had animated the men when they were first mobilized was not yet dead. Those for whom the *Marseillaise* was still a rallying-song had not ceased to link it with the cult of patriotism and the hatred of tyrants.

The trouble was that among the wage-earners these instincts, which were still strong, and which a less pusillanimous government would have known how to encourage, were at variance with certain other, and more recent, tendencies which were at work within the collective mind. I, with most of the men of my generation, had built enormous hopes, when we were young, on the trade-union movement. But we made no allowance for the narrowness of outlook which, little by little, choked the enthusiasm of the early, epic struggles. What was the cause of this failure? Partly, no doubt, an inevitable preoccupation with wage-claims, and a consequent scaling-down of interest and policy; partly, too, the fact that Labor's leaders allowed themselves to get tangled up in the old political game of electoral propaganda and lobbying. However that may be, it is true to say that the trade-union movement has shown a growing tendency everywhere to diverge from the road on which its feet were originally set, as though dogged by some ineluctable Fate.

Everyone knows that word *kleinburgerlich* with which Marx stig-
matized all politico-social movements which confined themselves
to the narrow field of partial interests. Could anything have been
more *kleinburgerlich,* more *petit bourgeois,* than the attitude
adopted in the last few years, and even during the war, by most of
the big unions, and especially by those which included civil servants
in their ranks? I have attended not a few meetings of my own
professional organization. Its members were drawn from the intellectual class, but it is true to say that scarcely ever did they show real
concern for anything except—not money on a large scale, but what
I may call the small change of remuneration. They seemed to be
blissfully unaware of such problems as the role which our corpora-
tion might play in the life of the country; nor were they ever prepared
to discuss the bigger question of France's material future. Their
vision was limited to immediate issues of petty profit, and I am afraid
that this blindness marked the conduct of most of the big unions. I
saw something of the way in which the Post Office workers and the
railwaymen behaved both during and after the war, and the spectacle
was not a very edifying one. Most of them, I am sure, were very
decent fellows; a few, as events showed, could on occasion conduct
themselves like heroes. But is it by any means certain that the rank
and file, and, what is more important, their representatives, ever
really understood that the days through which we were living called
for more than parish-pump politics? Did they, I mean, fully realize
what was demanded of them in pursuance of their daily work? That,
after all, is the touchstone of the professional conscience. In most
cities of western France during the month of June I saw hordes of
wretched men wandering about the streets in an effort to get back
to their homes. All of them were carrying loads far heavier than they
could cope with, and why? Simply because the railway stations had
seen fit to close their left-luggage offices for fear of imposing on their
staffs a few hours of overtime, or of rather heavier work than usual.
It was this kind of short-sightedness, this kind of administrative
bumbledom, the effect of petty rivalry and refusal to get the last
ounce out of their members, which explains the nervelessness of
the trade-union movement all over Europe, and not least in France,
when confronted by the first aggressive moves of the dictator states.
It accounts for their war record. What did a few noisy "resolutions,"

aimed at the gallery, matter? The point is that the general run of organized labor never got into their heads that the only thing that counted was as complete and as rapid a victory as possible for their country, and the defeat, not only of Nazism, but of all those elements of its philosophy which its imitators, in the event of success, would inevitably borrow. They had not been taught, as they should have been by leaders worthy of the name, to look above, beyond, and around the petty problems of every day. By concentrating attention on matters with the earning of their daily bread, they ran the risk of discovering that there might be no daily bread to earn. And now the hour of doom has sounded. Seldom has shortsightedness been more harshly punished. . . . Thus it came about that though the general needs of our national defense were more inextricably than ever bound up with the interests of the wage-earners, they made demands upon the working class which, however legitimately obvious they may have been, were compromised by a spirit of uncertainty and gloom in the factories. This vague lack of purpose was bad enough; it was made far worse by the incredible contradictions of French Communism. . . .

Every conceivable sin is laid at the door of the political regime which governed France in the years before the war. I have only to look about me to feel convinced that the parliamentary system has too often favored intrigue at the cost of intelligence and true loyalty. . . . It was entirely owing to our ministers and our assemblies that we were so ill prepared for war. Of that there can be not the slightest doubt. Not, it is true, that the High Command did much to help them. But nothing shed a cruder light on the spinelessness of Government than its capitulation to the technicians. In 1915 a succession of Parliamentary Commissions did more to provide us with heavy artillery than did all the artillerymen put together. Why did not their successors do more, and do it quicker, in the matter of airplanes and tanks? The history of the Ministry of Munitions reads like a lesson in unreason. It is incredible that we should have had to wait until the war was several months old before it was even set up, and then only as a makeshift organization. It should have been ready to start work, with a staff already picked and prepared, on the very day that mobilization was ordered. Only very exceptionally did Parliament ever refuse credits if the specialists demanded them with sufficient firmness, but it lacked the power to compel their proper use. It could, had it so wished, have put its hand in the elector's pocket, but it was afraid of irritating him. Its dislike of imposing on reservists the necessary period of field-training undermined the whole principle of the nation at arms. True, the routine of the barrack-square—not the best way of utilizing these periods of instruction—did at least set that particular ball rolling, but that is not saying much. More than once the leaders of the Government found themselves driven to ask for extraordinary powers—which was tantamount to admitting that the constitutional machinery was getting rusty. It would have been far better to redesign the machine while there was yet time. Those extraordinary powers were the line of least resistance, though nobody seems to have realized that they merely served to reinforce the existing practices of government and did nothing towards reforming them. Spoiled by a long familiarity with the lobbies, our political leaders imagined that they were gleaning information when all they were doing was to collect gossip from chance acquaintances. All problems, of the world as well as of the nation, appeared to them in the light of personal rivalries.

That the system suffered from weaknesses there can be no denying; but it was not so inherently vicious as has sometimes been argued. Many of the crimes of which it has been accused were, I should say, purely imaginary. It is often said that party, and in particular, anti-clerical, passions disorganized the armed forces. I can bear witness from my own experience that at Bohain General Blanchard went to Mass every Sunday. To assume that he had waited until war broke out to do so would be to level a gratuitous insult at his civic courage. It was right and proper that he, as a believer, should publicly perform his religious duties. The unbeliever who held such acts against him showed himself to be a fool or a boor. But I see no reason to maintain that those religious convictions loyally adhered to, stood in the way of his being given an army by a succession of so-called Left-Wing governments, or of his leading it to defeat.

Did those parliaments of ours, if it comes to that, or the ministries born of them, ever really concentrate the government of the country in their own hands? Earlier systems had left a legacy of public corporations which the politicians never really succeeded in controlling.

No doubt party considerations did to some extent weigh in the appointment of the heads of these bodies, and, as the winds of the moment blew, so did personalities change—not always with the happiest results. But, fundamentally, these great organizations were self-governing, and the men who formed their rank and file always remained, roughly, of the same type. The Ecole des Sciences Politiques, for instance, was always the spiritual home of scions of rich and powerful families. Its graduates filled the embassies, the Treasury, the Council of State, and the Public Audit Office. The Ecole Polytechnique, with its curious power of leaving an indelible and recognizable imprint on the young men who had passed through it, did far more than supply recruits for the general staffs of industry. It unlocked the door to a career in public engineering, where promotion had almost the automatic precision of a well-oiled machine. The universities, through the medium of a complex arrangement of councils and committees, filled any vacancies there might be in their teaching-staffs by a system of co-option which was not without its dangers when the need for new blood arose, and could offer to their successful students guarantees of permanent employment which the system at present in force has—provisionally, it is said—abolished. The Institute of France, entrenched in its wealth and in that prestige which the glitter of a title can always impose even on those who pass for being philosophically minded, still retains, for good or ill, the full dignity of its intellectual pre-eminence. If the Academy might occasionally be influenced in its elections by political considerations, it can scarcely be maintained that these have been of a Left-Wing kind. "I know of only three citadels of Conservatism," said Paul Bourget on one occasion, "the House of Lords, the German General Staff, and the French Academy."

Was the regime right or wrong in the consideration it habitually showed to these ancient corporations? The subject might be discussed endlessly. Some will uphold them in the interests of stability and in recognition of an honorable tradition. Others, with whom, I confess, my own sympathies lie, will argue against them on grounds of bureaucratic tendencies, routine mentality, and professional arrogance. . . .

But what, more than anything else, has injured our machinery of State, and, literally, stopped it from working, is that major lack of understanding which lies like a blight over the minds of almost all Frenchmen.

It is a good thing, and a sign of health, that those in a free country who represent contrasted social theories should freely air their differences. Society today being what it is, class interests are bound to be at odds. Antagonisms there must be, and it is well that they should be recognized. It is only when this stage of social friction ceases to be regarded as normal and legitimate that the country as a whole begins to suffer.

More than once in the course of this book I have made use of the word *bourgeoisie*—not without a qualm of conscience. The sciences which have human beings as their subject are, at best, but empirical, and their pursuit is made more than ever difficult when they are cluttered up with words which have become so debased by long use that their meaning has ceased to be clear. The realities which they express are too complex; the language which expresses them too fluid. That, however, is beyond our power to alter. Until some better means of communication than that of language has been evolved, we must resign ourselves to using the only vocabulary which the imperfections of our tongue have made available. But it can be used successfully only if we define our terms. Let me say, then, that, when speaking of Frenchmen I employ the term *bourgeois,* I mean someone who is not dependent for his livelihood on the work of his hands; whose income, irrespective of its source and of its size (for it may vary considerably from individual to individual), permits him to live in easy circumstances, and gives him a sense of security such as no mere wage-earner can ever know in his own hazardous existence; whose education, enjoyed from birth, if his family happens to be an old-established one, or gained in the course of an exceptional rise in the social scale, is richer in texture, better in quality, and more pretentious in kind than the minimum cultural training enjoyed by the ordinary man in the street. Finally, the *bourgeois* is a man who believes that he belongs to a class which is marked out for leadership in the country's affairs, and, by a thousand little details of dress, language, and good manners, shows more or less instinctively that he is one of a very special group and enjoys a high degree of prestige in the eyes of less fortunate mortals.

Now, the *bourgeoisie,* thus defined, was not feeling any too happy in pre-war France. The economic changes which it was the fashion to lay at the door of the last world catastrophe, though some of them had other causes, were in process of sapping the foundations of those solid, unadventurous fortunes which had existed in earlier days when an income from investments had formed the sole resource of many families, and was the goal of many others whose members were just beginning to climb the ladder of success. In the world brought into existence by the first war, this kind of livelihood was beginning to melt away in the hands of its astonished possessors. The workers were setting their faces stubbornly against all attempts to reduce wages, with the result that after each recurrent crisis, profits and dividends alike grew smaller. The spread of industry in new countries which showed an increasing tendency to become self-sufficient was producing an ever-worsening condition of anemia in the capitalistic system not only of France but of Europe generally. The aggressive mood of the newcomers to the social scene was already threatening the economic and political power of a group which had long been accustomed to command, and had conveniently come to terms with the institutions of a democracy to which many of its members had even sworn allegiance. As usually happens, custom had lagged behind fact. The franchise had been widened to include workers on the land and in the factories, but the exercise of the vote had not as yet seriously shaken the traditional position of superiority enjoyed, outside the capital, by the bigwigs of the middle class. Indeed, to some extent it benefited them, because they were able, partially at least, to eliminate from the great offices of state their old adversaries of the great noble and near-noble families. Untouched by aristocratic arrogance, their outlook on life was genuinely humanistic, and it drew strength from a democratic system so long as that system did not strike at them through their pockets or undermine the solid structure of their very real, though modest prestige. But a day soon came when the voters of the lowest category, encouraged in their demands by the economic tragedy of the times, began to make their voices heard. And what those voices now expressed was something that was a great deal more dangerous than it had formerly been. Old resentments drew fresh vigor from an exacerbated sense of inequality. The *bourgeois,* forced to realize that he had got to work a good deal harder than he had done in the past, got the ideas that the "masses," whose labor was, in the last analysis, the source of his own profits, were working less—which was true, and even less than he was—which was not, perhaps, equally true, and certainly did not take into account the difference in degree of human fatigue. He grew indignant at the thought that the manual worker had now enough free time to enable him to go to the cinema like his boss. The workers' attitude to money, born of a long past of insecurity which had firmly fixed in their minds the conviction that it was useless to look ahead, and that the morrow could be left to take care of itself, offended his inborn respect for the virtue of saving. Even the most charitable-minded sought in vain among the crowds parading with clenched fists raised, and demanding their rights with a violence which, in fact, was no more than a rather crude expression of honest frankness, the "respectable poor" who had peopled with such deferential charm the novels of Madame de Ségur. The value of discipline, of docile good nature, of a ready acceptance of social differences by the less fortunate, had formed the basis of their timid and unadventurous education. And now it looked as though all these things were to be swept away for good and all. With them, they felt, would go something far more valuable, that sense of the common weal which, little though the comfortably off might think it, does demand a greater degree of sacrifice from the poor than from the rich.

Because, for all these reasons, the members of the *bourgeoisie* had grown anxious and discontented, they now began to show signs of bitterness. They might, had they looked a little closer, have reached a better understanding of the "People" from whom they were themselves sprung, and with whom they had more than one deep affinity. But because they were unused to making the mental effort which social analysis demands, they preferred to condemn out of hand. It would be difficult to exaggerate the sense of shock felt by the comfortable classes, and even by men who had a reputation for liberal-mindedness, at the coming of the Popular Front in 1936. All those who had a few pennies to bless themselves with smelled the rising wind of disaster, and the good housewife was, if anything, more terrified than her husband. It is the fashion today to say that the Jews were behind the Left-Wing movement. Poor Synagogue—always fated to act as scapegoat! I know, from what I saw with my own eyes, that it trembled even more violently than the

Church. The same held true of the non-Catholic congregations. "The old Protestant employer's a thing of the past"—I heard a writer say who had been brought up in Nonconformist circles. "At one time no one could have been more whole-heartedly concerned for the well-being of his people than he was, but now he is among the most rancorous of their critics." A deep fissure was opening almost before our eyes in the fabric of French social life. The country was splitting into two opposed groups.

It is no part of my intention to enter the lists as a champion of the Popular Front governments. They are dead now, and those who for a moment put their faith in them may, perhaps, be allowed to cast a handful of dust in pious memory on their graves. More than this they do not deserve. They fell without glory, and what makes it worse is that their adversaries had little to do with their overthrow. Events outstripped them, but even that is not the whole story. The movement failed mainly because of the follies of its supporters, or of those who claimed to be its supporters. Still, the attitude of the greater part of middle-class opinion was inexcusable. It grumbled with stupid mulishness at everything that was done, whether good or bad. One decent fellow of my acquaintance obstinately refused to set foot inside the Exposition Universelle. He liked looking at beautiful things, and it offered for his enjoyment an incomparable display of the glories of French art. But that made not the slightest difference. It was enough for him that a detested minister had officiated at the opening ceremony! It was said that the demands of organized labor, at one moment, had raised doubts as to its being ready in time, and that was enough to put it outside the pale. And what an outcry there was when the authorities began to talk about the organization of leisure! The idea was greeted with mockery, and attempts were even made to bring it to nothing. Yet the very people who took that attitude then are now prepared to extol to the skies similar efforts, made more or less seriously, though under a different name, by regimes after their own hearts. . . .

As a result of attacking the regime, these same *bourgeois* proceeded, naturally, to condemn the nation which had produced it. Driven to despair of their own future, they ended by despairing of their country. If anyone be tempted to say that I exaggerate, let him re-read the newspapers on which, a few years ago, the middle classes lived, and whose outlook they dictated. He will find the experience edifying. At the time when Belgium had just rejected the offer of an alliance in favor of a neutrality which unhappily turned out to be fallacious, a friend of mine in Brussels said: "You've no idea of the amount of damage done to the French cause by your great Weeklies. They declare in every issue that France, as a nation, is in an advanced stage of putrescence. Well, I'm afraid we believe 'em. How can you expect us not to?" We ourselves believed them only too well. Many men of what might still claim to be our ruling classes, since from them were drawn our leaders of industry, our senior civil servants, the majority of our reserve officers, set off for the war haunted by those gloomy prognostications. They were taking their orders from a political set-up which they held to be hopelessly corrupt. They were defending a country which they did not seriously think could offer any genuine resistance. The soldiers under their command were the sons of that "People" which they were only too glad to regard as degenerate. No matter how high their own courage, no matter how resolute their own patriotism, it can hardly be maintained that this was the best intellectual preparation for men who would be called upon to fight "to the last quarter of an hour."

Now, those who provided the personnel for the various military staffs were only too ready to share these jaundiced points of view. I do not mean that they were all to the same extent contaminated. It was by no means true that *all* regular officers, even those in the most senior positions, necessarily belonged to the world of hereditary wealth. More than one, on the contrary, hailed from a social level which was little, if at all, removed from that of the great mass of his countrymen. By the nature of their calling, and as a point of honor, they were for the most part strangers to the petty outlook of the tradesman. The future of capitalism—supposing that they ever had time to think about such things—would not have caused them any particular concern, and most of them would have been left unmoved by the prospect of a redistribution of the national wealth. Almost all of them were men with a strong sense of duty, fervent patriots, and very conscious that they were soldiers of France. The idea that they might be regarded as the mercenaries of certain private interests, or of any one class, would have brought a blush of shame to their cheeks. But what did they know of social realities? Education, the spirit of caste, tradition, had all combined to build around them a wall of ignorance and error. Their thoughts were simple. The "Left" meant for them "anti-militarism," free thought, and a hatred of that authority which, as everyone knows, is the main source of an army's strength. About Socialists they had long known all there was to know. They equated the word with the "bad" soldier, the man who always has a grouse, and, horror of horrors, sometimes communicates his grievances to the Press. Anyone who had dealings with "Socialists" became automatically suspect. Even Roosevelt had something of the "Bolshie" about him (I actually heard that said once by a highly placed staff officer). They were not, as a whole, intellectually curious, and they had been trained from boyhood to flee from heresy as from the plague. This brief and simple orthodoxy was admirably suited to their needs. They never made the slightest attempt to acquire information. Among the newspapers which lay on our anteroom table, *Le Temps* was, by comparison with its neighbors, a "red rag." And so it came about that a whole group of young leaders, recruited from among the most intelligent representatives of the nation, never opened a daily paper which reflected, even in the smallest degree, the opinions professed, rightly or wrongly, by the majority of Frenchmen.

There is no getting away from the fact that we, the teachers, were largely to blame for this state of affairs. I have long felt it to be deplorable that men whose proud boast it was in recent years that they stood for all that was most liberal, most disinterested, and most humanly progressive, in our country, should have been guilty of the serious charge of having made no effort whatever to touch the understanding of a professional body which enshrined such high moral values. Their failure to do so dates, I think, from the Dreyfus affair, and the original responsibility does not rest on the shoulders of those who, at that time, were on our side of the barricades. But that is no excuse for what has happened since. Many a time I have said to myself, as I saw my companions drinking in like harmless milk the poisonous brew compacted of stupidity and hatred which certain squalid sheets continued to dispense even during the war: "What a shame it is that such fine fellows should be so ill informed: what a crying scandal that no one has ever really tried to enlighten them."

The fact remains that we are now in a position to measure up the results. Ill informed about the infinite resources of a people that has remained far healthier than they, as the result of poisonous teaching, have been inclined to believe; rendered incapable by inherited contempt and by the limited routine of their training to call in time upon its inexhaustible reserves of strength, our leaders not only let themselves be beaten, but too soon decided that it was perfectly natural that they should be beaten. By laying down their arms before there was any real necessity for them to do so, they have assured the triumph of a faction. Some of them, to be sure, strove hard, by backing the coup d'état, to disguise their fault. But others there were, in the High Command and in almost every rank of the Army, who were very far from pursuing any such selfish design. They accepted the disaster, but with rage in their hearts. However that may be, they did accept it, and long before they need have done. They were ready to find consolation in the thought that beneath the ruins of France a shameful regime might be crushed to death, and that if they yielded it was to a punishment meted out by Destiny to a guilty nation.

The generation to which I belong has a bad conscience. It is true that we emerged from the last war desperately tired, and that after four years not only of fighting, but of mental laziness, we were only too anxious to get back to our proper employments and take up the tools that we had left to rust upon the benches. So behindhand were we with our work that we set ourselves to bolt it down in indigestible mouthfuls. That is our excuse. But I have long ceased to believe that it can wash us clean of guilt. . . .

The duty of reconstructing our country will not fall on the shoulders of my generation. France in defeat will be seen to have had a Government of old men. That is but natural. France of the new springtime must be the creation of the young. As compared with their elders of the last war, they will have one sad privilege: they will not have to guard against the lethargy bred of victory. Whatever form the final triumph may take, it will be many years before the stain of 1940 can be effaced. It may be a good thing that these young people will have to work in a white heat of rage. It would be impertinent on my part to outline a program for them. They will search for the laws of the future in the intimacy of their heads and of their hearts. The map of the future will be drawn as a result of the lessons they have learned. All I beg of them is that they shall avoid the dry inhumanity of systems which, from rancor or from pride, set themselves to rule the mass of their countrymen without providing them with adequate instruction, without being in true communion with them. Our people deserve to be trusted, to be taken into the confidence of their leaders. I hope, too, that though they may do new things, many new things, they will not break the links that bind us to our authentic heritage, which is not at all, or, at least, not wholly, what some self-styled apostles of tradition have imagined it to be. On one occasion Hitler said to Rauschning: "It is very much better to bank on the vices of men than on their virtues. The French Revolution appealed to virtue. We shall be better advised to do the contrary." A Frenchman, that is to say, a civilized man—for the two are identical—will be forgiven if he substitutes for this teaching that of the Revolution and of Montesquieu: "A State founded on the People needs a mainspring: and that mainspring is virtue." What matter if the task is thereby made more difficult—as it will be? A free people in pursuit of noble ends runs a double risk. But are soldiers on the field of battle to be warned against the spirit of adventure?

Suggestions for Additional Reading

The best introduction to the historiography of the fall of France is John C. Cairns' article, "Along the Road Back to France, 1940," *American Historical Review*, LXIV (April 1959). Another short but useful introduction to the problem is Saul K. Padover's "France Today," *Social Research*, XVI (December 1949).

There are four recent accounts of the events of May-June 1940: Guy Chapman, *Why France Fell: The Defeat of the French Army in 1940* (New York, Chicago & San Francisco, 1968); Alistair Horne, *To Lose a Battle, France 1940* (Boston, 1969); William L. Shirer, *The Collapse of the Third Republic: An Inquiry into the Fall of France in 1940* (New York, 1969); and John Williams, *The Ides of May: The Defeat of France, May-June, 1940* (New York, 1968). The most ambitious of these, William Shirer's massive work, is valuable chiefly for its eyewitness accounts by a keen observer. The other three concentrate on military operations. Publishers' claims to the contrary, the analysis in depth of the political, social and economic factors leading to the debacle of 1940 has yet to be written.

While they are not as revealing as one might have wished, the findings of the *Commission d'Enquête Parlementaire sur les événements survenus en France de 1933 à 1945,* 2 vols. of reports, 9 vols. of documents (Paris, 1951–1954) contain much valuable material. The *French Yellow Book: Diplomatic Documents, 1938–1939* (New York, 1940) presents the events leading to the final crisis of September 1939 from the standpoint of the French government. The whole question of responsibilities for the war is ably reviewed in another volume of the *Problems in European Civilization* series, *The Outbreak of the Second World War—Design or Blunder?,* ed. John L. Snell (Boston, 1963).

The pronouncements, memoirs, and apologias of the leading actors in the drama still constitute the richest and most rewarding literature on the fall of France. See especially: Paul Reynaud, *In the Thick of the Fight, 1930–1945,* tr. James D. Lambert (New York, 1955) and *Mémoires: Envers et contre tous, 7 mars, 1936–16 juin, 1940* (Paris, 1964); Camille Chautemps, *Cahiers secrets de l'Armistice, 1939–1940* (Paris, 1964); Edouard Herriot, *Episodes, 1940–1944* (Paris, 1950); Léon Blum, *Mémoires. La Prison et le procès. A l'èchelle humaine, 1940–1945* (Paris, 1955); Pierre Cot, *Triumph of Treason,* trs. Sybille & Milton Crane (New York, 1944); Pierre-Etienne Flandin, *Politique française, 1919–1940* (Paris, 1947); General Gamelin, *Servir* (3 vols., Paris, 1946–1947); Maxime Weygand, *Recalled to Service: The Memoirs of General Maxime Weygand,* tr. E. W. Dickes (New York, 1952); Alain Darlan, *L'Amiral Darlan parle* (Paris, 1952); Pierre Laval, *Laval parle* (Paris, 1948); and Philippe Pétain, *Paroles aux Français: Messages et écrits, 1934–1941* (Lyon, 1941). Last but far from least, no serious student of the question can omit consulting the relevant chapters in *The Complete War Memoirs of Charles De Gaulle, 1940–1946* (New York, 1964) and Winston Churchill, *The Second World War* (6 vols., London, 1950–1955).

The following stand out among the many works dealing with the military aspects of the Battle of France: General Gamelin, *La Guerre: Septembre, 1939–Mai, 1940 (Servir,* III, Paris, 1947); General Louis Koeltz, *Comment s'est joué notre destin: Hitler et l'offensive du 10 mai, 1940* (Paris, 1957); and Major-General Sir Edward L. Spears, *The Fall of France, June 1940 (Assignment to Catastrophe,* II, London, 1953–1954). Spears was Churchill's personal envoy to the French government, and his account reveals more than the author perhaps intended on the state of Franco-British relations. The most challenging and controversial account of the Battle of France remains *Soixante jours qui ébranlèrent l'Occident: 10 mai–10 juillet, 1940* (3 vols., Paris, 1956), the work of Jacques Benoist-Méchin, an unrepentant former Vichyite and collaborationist. This work is now available in a one-volume English translation, *Sixty Days that Shook the West; The Fall of France, 1940,* tr. Peter Wiles (London & New York, 1963). Jacques Minart, *Le Drame du désarmement français (1918–1939)* (Paris, 1960), revives the thesis of an inadequately prepared France being led to the slaughter. Roland Dorgelès, *La Drôle de guerre, 1939–1940* (Paris, 1957), presents a series of vignettes of life at the front during the months of the phoney war; and Antoine de Saint-Exupéry, *Pilote de guerre* (New York, 1942), gives a gripping account of a French pilot's experience at the height of the German offensive.

The number and variety of works on the political aspects of the question serve as a reminder that the debacle of 1940 was far more than a millitary collapse. Good treatments of the demise of the Third Republic can be found in: Jacques Chastenet, *Le Drame final, 1938–1940 (Histoire de la Troisième République,* VII) (Paris, 1963); Emmanuel Beau de Loménie, *La Mort de la Troisième République* (Paris, 1951); André Siegfried, *De la IIIe à la IVe République* (Paris, 1956); Robert Aron, *The Vichy Regime 1940–1944,* tr. Humphrey Hare (New York, 1958); and Paul Farmer, *Vichy: Political Dilemma* (New York, 1955). Henri Amouroux, *Le 18 juin 1940* (Paris, 1964), is a fascinating, hour-by-hour account of the struggle between the partisans of the war *à outrance* and the advocates of an immediate armistice. Other studies stress the cause and effect relationship between the outcome of the Battle of France and the political atmosphere prevailing in the country at large. Charles Micaud, *The French Right and Nazi Germany* (Durham, N.C., 1943), traces the gradual attrition of the Right's martial fervor, while the early portions of Alexander Werth's *France: 1940–1955* (New York, 1956) reveal the damaging effects of the campaigns of the Extreme Right on the morale of the French nation. On the other side of the fence, A. Rossi's aforementioned *Les Communistes Français pendant la Drôle de Guerre* (Paris, 1951) is a severe, well-documented indictment of the role played by the Extreme Left. Jacques Madaule, "La France en Guerre," *Esprit*, VIII (February 1940), is a wartime commentary on pacifist and defeatist attitudes, General Marcel Boucherie, "Les Causes politiques et morales d'un désastre: 1940," *Revue de défense nationale,* XIV (March 1958), is the tempered verdict of an army defender.

Today, the chief value of the vast body of partisan literature is that it underlines the extreme bitterness of French political quarrels. For instance, Lucien Rebatet, *Les Décombres* (Paris, 1942), and Robert Brasillach, *Journal d'un homme occupé* (Paris, 1955) typify the extreme rightist mentality and point of view; and the anonymous pamphlet, *Pétain-Laval: The Conspiracy* (London, 1942), remains the classic exposition of the thesis that the country's defeat and the downfall of the Republic were caused by a deliberate plot engineered by the future leaders and supporters of the Vichy regime.

Léon Blum devant la Cour de Riom (Paris, 1945) and Pierre Mazé and Roger Génébrier, *Les Grandes journées du procès de Riom* (Paris, 1945), provide us with a convenient summary of the issues which continue to divide Frenchmen in the great debate over the causes and responsibilities for the fall of France.

Finally, a number of general works on modern France contain excellent short accounts of the crisis of 1939–1940, and attempt to place the debacle in the proper historical context. Of these, the following will be consulted with special profit: D. W. Brogan, *The French Nation from Napoleon to Pétain: 1814–1940* (New York, 1957); René Albrecht-Carrié, *France, Europe and the Two World Wars* (Geneva, 1960); Gordon Wright, *France in Modern Times: 1760 to the Present* (Chicago, 1960); Paul Gagnon, *France Since 1789* (New York, 1964); Ernest John Knapton, *France: An Interpretive History* (New York, 1971); and Stanley Hoffman *et al., In Search of France* (Cambridge, Mass., 1963). The editor's own thesis is developed in "The Third Republic in Historical Perspective," chapter II of Gerald N. Grob, ed., *Statesmen and Statecraft of the Modern West: Essays in Honor of Dwight E. Lee and H. Donaldson Jordan* (Barre, Mass., 1967).